Catherine Collins, RSCJ
(1937 – 2010)

Catherine Collins, RSCJ (1937 – 2010)

Innovator with Heart and Vision

Jan Dunn, RSCJ

CATHERINE COLLINS, RSCJ (1937 – 2010)
INNOVATOR WITH HEART AND VISION

iUniverse books may be ordered through booksellers or by contacting:

iUniverse
1663 Liberty Drive
Bloomington, IN 47403
www.iuniverse.com
844-349-9409

ISBN: 978-1-6632-2549-8 (sc)
ISBN: 978-1-6632-2550-4 (e)

Library of Congress Control Number: 2021915313

Print information available on the last page.

iUniverse rev. date: 07/27/2021

Contents

Introduction .. vii

Early Life ... 1
Final Vows ... 9
Early Professed Life .. 17
Headmistress of Stone Ridge .. 18
Origins of the Network ... 24
Goals and Criteria .. 32
Society Seminar .. 39
Development of the Network .. 43
Meetings of Heads of Schools .. 45
Contribution to the International Society ... 48
International Visits .. 50
International Society Involvement .. 58
International Education Commission ... 61
Center for Educational Design and Communication 67
Leadership in the Province ... 84
A Visionary ... 88

Contents

Introduction

The life of Catherine (Kit) Collins spanned the period of renewal of religious life called for by the Second Vatican Council. A brilliant innovator, Kit always saw possibilities. She spent the greater part of her life creating, implementing, and developing two major structures in what would eventually become the United States – Canada Province of the Society of the Sacred Heart: the Network of Sacred Heart Schools and the Center for Educational Design, now called the Stuart Center, in Washington, D.C.

Out-going and gregarious, Kit was a creative person who had an idea a minute. She was, as is said, "a mover and shaker," and her ideas play out still in many arenas related to social justice and communication; but perhaps her most lasting influence is the networking she began among the schools, which now has gone well beyond the United States to schools all over the world that have emulated the model of networking and used some of Kit's ideas for organizing, technological idea-sharing, and self-evaluation.

I am grateful for the many who shared their stories of Kit to make this biography possible. I am especially grateful to her family, to Betsy Hartson, RSCJ, her friend and long-time community member, to Tracey Gray who worked with her at the Morino Institute, and the staff at the Center, and to many fellow educators in the Network.

Her legacy teaches us to live into the future with hope and courage.

Catherine Collins, RSCJ, (called Kit) was a creative genius. She was an original thinker and innovator who led the Society of the Sacred Heart in the U.S.A. and internationally into new, uncharted territory. Her keen mind coupled with her boundless energy fueled her action. When she entered a room, she enveloped it and marked others by her effervescent personality. Never satisfied with the status quo, Kit not only saw possibilities but also created them. She was a dynamic leader who fearlessly forged new paths on which others followed her. But, primarily, Kit was a Religious of the Sacred Heart who strove to make known the love of the Heart of Christ all her life.

On an evening in early March 2015, five years after Kit's death, a group of Religious of the Sacred Heart gathered in the living room of the Otis Street community in Washington where Kit had lived for many years. Surrounding them were artifacts that Kit had brought the community from her trip to Africa in the 1970s. The sisters gathered to remember Kit, to share reflections on her life and legacy. Words and phrases poured forth to describe this extraordinary woman: "resourceful, knew what she wanted, dynamic, full of life and energy, strong, good conversationalist, opinionated." Ellen Nelson[1] described her as a "mentor," an active member of the Society who always exhibited "hope in the Society." Helen McCulloch[2] remembered as a novice meeting Kit when she visited the novitiate in Boston to see her dearest friends—Mickey McKay[3] who was in charge of the novices, and Ronnie Dewey[4] and Nance O'Neil,[5] both former provincials. Others in the gathering that evening remembered Kit as "entertaining, kind,

[1] Ellen Nelson, RSCJ, born in in Grand Rapids, Michigan, on 8/18/1947, now lives in Washington, D.C.

[2] Helen McCulloch, RSCJ, born in Pittsfield, Massachusetts, on 2/7/1943, lives and works in Washington, D.C.

[3] Mary Catherine "Mickey" McKay was born in 1929 in Indianapolis, Indiana, but grew up in Vermont; she was a member of the General Council from 1970 to 1976. She served later as mistress of novices but also spent time in Nicaragua, and in her later years gave retreats in various provinces of the Society. She died unexpectedly in 2001 while giving a workshop to the Japanese province.

[4] Rosemary "Ronnie" Dewey, RSCJ, born in Chicago on 8/18/1929, was provincial of the Chicago Province.

[5] Nance O'Neil, RSCJ, born on 3/10/1928 in Cleveland, Ohio, served as provincial of the New York Province, then became the first provincial of the Province of the United States, which combined the previous five provinces. In 1989, she founded the Society's mission in Indonesia, where she still serves.

and generous," as well as an ardent "discount shopper who traveled miles to find a bargain."

Helen McCulloch emphasized that Kit was a leader in the Society at all levels. Locally, Kit served as area director of the Washington, D.C., area of the Religious of the Sacred Heart. Nationally in the U.S., Kit began the Network of Sacred Heart Schools, and internationally, she chaired the International Education Commission (IEC). She facilitated international chapters (general meetings of the Society). Kit travelled the world giving talks on education and on the mission of the Society and the Network in the U.S. Her influence in the international Society was marked not only by her enthusiasm for education, but also by her desire for a global outlook, social analysis, and a drive for social justice. She was summed up as a person who was always "reading, thinking, and learning."

Kit Collins was indeed a genius and an innovator who shared her talents with others with decisiveness and humor! Kit "knew how to work and how to play," remembered Betsy Hartson,[6] her lifetime friend who lived with Kit for many years. "Her Irish eyes sparkled as she pushed us all to new horizons and heights!" This phrase sums up Kit's life and legacy; she pushed all to "new horizons and heights."

[6] Elizabeth "Betsy" Hartson, RSCJ, was born in New Orleans on 12/27/1937. She taught there for many years and subsequently moved to Washington, D.C., where she founded an alternative GED program for adults.

Early Life

"Kit" Collins, christened Catherine Cecilia, was born on April 14, 1937, in Boston, Massachusetts. As a Bostonian, Kit "pahked the cah," and drank "wah-ter" all her life; but when she entered the Society of the Sacred Heart, the whole world became her home, and she left her mark on it.

Her parents, James Francis Collins and Esther McCafferty, were Irish immigrants. Kit was the middle child of five. She had three brothers—George, Joseph, and James—and a sister, Paula.

The Collins family

The family was lively, and joy abounded in the home. They loved one another, delighting in being together. Kit's devotion to her family continued throughout her life. She was ever faithful to her parents and loved her brothers and sisters and their children. "Aunt Kit" doted on

her nieces and nephews, and eventually, on their children as well. Kit's family returned the feeling. Both circumstances tore at Kit's heart and called out her compassion. She acted as a surrogate mother to her nieces and nephews. Fran de la Chapelle,[7] who lived with Kit in the Upstairs community on Newton Academy's campus,[8] recalled how Kit's nieces and nephews would visit and make cookies with Catherine Riley[9] who lived in the community. When Sister de la Chapelle, as dean of students at Newton College, needed a doctor to attend school touch-football games, Kit's brother Joe graciously obliged. Kit, Joe, and Fran enjoyed these games together. Her brother, Joe, according to Georgie Blaeser,[10] was the light of Kit's life, but she was equally devoted to her sister Polly.

Kit had a gift of laughter that delighted the whole group. For her first Christmas in the novitiate at Kenwood, the family was allowed to send her one present, which Kit discovered on her chair in the community room on Christmas morning. Meg Canty,[11] a friend who had entered the convent with Kit, recalls that first Christmas in the novitiate, "We were each allowed to receive one gift and, Christmas morning, there was a single present on each of our chairs. Kit received a pogo stick and spent the following few minutes entertaining all of us by jumping around the room." Kit "lightened everyone's spirit." Kit's humor was a gift passed down from her parents. As an example, after the funeral Mass for her father, who died on July 3, 1975, Kit and her family were waiting in the limousine for the drive to the cemetery. Suddenly, there was banging on the window, and an intoxicated mourner declared to Mrs. Collins that "Joe was one of the best men I ever knew and would certainly be blessed." Mrs. Collins graciously acknowledged him. When she rolled up the window, she turned to the family and said, "I loved that man for so many years, and I never knew his name was Joe." Kit's father's name was James. The family who had been dissolved in tears

[7] Frances "Fran" de la Chapelle, RSCJ, was born in Englewood, New Jersey, on 2/3/1940 and serves as ministry coordinator for the USC province.

[8] Newton Country Day School, Newton, Massachusetts

[9] Catherine Riley, RSCJ, was born in Albany, New York, on 9/10/1914. She lived in Newton, Massachusetts for many years and knew Kit well.

[10] Georgie Blaeser, RSCJ, born in Chicago on 1/30/1940, worked in Network schools, served on the provincial team and in the secretariat at the motherhouse; she was on the staff at Sprout Creek Farm, where she died on 6/1/2016.

[11] Margaret "Meg" Canty, RSCJ, was born in New York on 9/8/1934, formerly taught and administered in Network schools and now lives in one of the retirement communities in Albany.

moments earlier was now laughing uncontrollably, so much so that the limousine began to shake.

Kit attended public school in Belmont, Massachusetts. She was a good student and thoroughly enjoyed learning. Curious by nature, she particularly loved literature and history. Her grades reflected this interest. Her fascination with places and with people followed her throughout her life, as she traveled the globe and met and influenced so many people all around it. When Kit was a junior in high school, she transferred to Newton Country Day School of the Sacred Heart. Those two years at Newton changed her life, because there she met the Society of the Sacred Heart. She wrote, "I have a very special place in my grateful heart for what was implanted in me as a student of the Sacred Heart."

Kit at school (undated)

Graduating from Newton in 1954, Kit went on to Manhattanville College of the Sacred Heart in Purchase, New York, for four years, double majoring in psychology and theology. Kit's senior essay, entitled, *What About Juvenile Delinquency*, mirrored one of her lifelong passions—social justice! She wrote:

> In this paper, I have met and even attempted to love all the aspects of juvenile delinquency, for it is a field so large that one small paper can only hit on a few ideas. Because of this, I have looked at the problem and tried to throw efforts mainly into the field of education for causes and cures of

one of our nation's greatest and most important problems—
Juvenile Delinquency.

She received an A.

College friends remembered her as a good student, but one who knew how to enjoy herself. They remembered that Kit was able to "shoot pins into any form of pomposity," while always accepting others in a non-judgmental way. According to her friends, her sense of humor was one of her dominant and memorable virtues.

Kit in college

Despite parental opposition, after college Kit entered the Society of the Sacred Heart at Kenwood in Albany, New York, on September 7, 1958. She had kept her religious vocation a secret even from her roommate. Her friend Meg Canty said,

> Life in the noviceship was daunting, because life inside was totally different from life outside. There were rules, structures, and schedules to be observed, and all was done in silence! Even taking a bath at night was a ritual. My first real memory of the twelve of us who came that day was of all of us going down to the basement in an old elevator to take a shower. We turned up in bathrobes of various designs. Mine was a dainty, light blue quilted material. Then Kit appeared in hers, a full-length leopard print! The older novice (archangel) running the Otis elevator reminded

us we were to be in silence. As she turned and faced the elevator door, Kit raised her hand, as if it were a leopard's paw, and mouthed a silent "roar." We were laughing—in silence—until the "archangel" turned around. We resumed our solemn stance, and so it went several times, as we slowly descended to the basement. Because of Kit, the leopard, the laughter, and the new silence, we were bonded in a way that reality and memory cannot affect.

Kit wrote her parents as often as she was allowed, giving them what details she could share of her life at Kenwood. In August 1959, Kit wrote about the grape season that was about to begin. At that time, the novitiate kept a large vegetable garden, kept bees, and tended a grape arbor. Kit's letter highlighted that she is not, by inclination or nature, a farmer!

> The grape season is not far off now—and I can't forget how I spent it last fall laboring in the vineyard—and, of course, treading the winepress! Nasty things, we go to such pains to rescue every grape from every vine—and what happens!— they just come right back the next fall. I tell you it's a losing battle…. Well folks, I 'gots to go' now—if you get any news 'fix it up' and pass it along.
>
> In the meanwhile, be good—I am trying!
>
> Much, much love in CJM [Hearts of Jesus and Mary], Kit Collins

A new and very different experience for a city girl from Boston!

Kit on the day she received the religious habit

After professing her first vows on March 20, 1961, Kit spent a year in the juniorate, a period of study for novices and new aspirants.[12] She was then assigned to Eden Hall, a boarding school in Philadelphia, where she taught high school classes in English, history, philosophy, and religion. Vicky Rajca,[13] one of her early pupils, proclaimed that Kit "was the best teacher I ever had. She pushed me to go beyond what I thought I could do."

[12] Young religious who were not yet finally professed were called aspirants.
[13] Vicky Racja, RSCJ, born in Philadelphia on 6/8/1947, currently works at the Stuart Center; she knew Kit most of her life.

6

Kit at work in the classroom

Kit at the blackboard

During the summers at Eden Hall, Kit studied for her Master of Arts in Education at Manhattanville College. In 1965, she received the degree with a joint major in English and philosophy.

At the end of her aspirantship, the five years between first vows and final profession, Kit suffered a heart attack. She was twenty-nine years old. Lolín Menéndez[14] recalls meeting Kit for the first time and

[14] Lolín Menéndez, RSCJ, was born in San Juan, Puerto Rico, on 1/19/1943 and ministers in Puerto Rico.

realizing that Kit would never let her condition deter her from living a full life.

> I first met Kit Collins at Reverend Mother Bodkin's[15] funeral at Kenwood. I remember distinctly how she stood out in a very crowded dining room. The novices from the Washington Vicariate gravitated to her as if pulled by a magnet. She was young, good looking, exuding vitality and wit. She regaled us with stories of her heart attack at Eden Hall and her stay at Nazareth Hospital, where she was told that on Christmas day the sheets of only terminal cases were changed...so she determined that she would *not* be terminal...not for a while! I think she was twenty-six [actually twenty-nine] at the time, and lived with her "bad" heart, as she called it, never making an issue of it.

While the heart attack forever marked her, Kit was determined to lead a "normal life," unwilling to allow it to slow her down or delay her making final vows. In fact, she wrote letters to the superiors that she was well and able to follow the whole probation[16] program. While the attack did not prevent her from going to probation, Mary Jane Ferrier[17] later mused that it might have been the cause for Kit's night owl tendencies: "Perhaps Kit was afraid to go to sleep, lest she not wake up in the morning." Being a night owl would characterize her life until the end.

[15] Gertrude Bodkin, RSCJ, was born in 1875 in Rothkeale, Co. Limerick, Ireland. She entered the Society of the Sacred Heart at Roehampton, England, in 1894. She was mistress of novices at Kenwood, 1909-1931, and superior-vicar of the New York Vicariate, 1931-1953. She died at Kenwood in 1966.

[16] Probation is the name given to the period of preparation for final profession in the Society.

[17] Mary Jane Ferrier, RSCJ, born 7/18/1932, in Ottawa, taught in both Montreal and Vancouver, later became a psychotherapist. She lived with Kit in the Washington Provincial House.

Final Vows

In probation, the period of preparation for final profession at the motherhouse in Rome, Kit prayed to be receptive to God's grace and an instrument of God's love and goodness throughout her life. Her Lenten practice that year was twofold: care in prayer and "to help others with great fraternal kindness." Kit made that phrase her guide for the rest of her life.

During her months in Rome as a probanist, Vatican Council II closed. The Council ushered in many changes in the Church and in religious life. One of the most obvious changes was the transition from the traditional habit of the nuns to something more modern and less restrictive. Kit described the new habit as, "Very trim and certainly religious looking, and no driving problem." Driving was of particular concern, because the original cap closed off the sides of the face, making it impossible to see sideways and therefore dangerous for driving.

In Kit's probation group, seventeen different nationalities were represented, but the language of the probation was French, the. All conferences, instructions, and informal gatherings were conducted in French. During this period of preparation for final vows, Kit served as secretary to Reverend Mother Mary Elizabeth Tobin,[18] the American assistant general.

Kit entered into the spiritual preparation for her final vows with a deep, idealistic fervor. Her letters to her mother and father and others, as well as her notes during this time of preparation, testify to her love of and pride in the Society.

[18] Mary Elizabeth Tobin, RSCJ, born in Albany, New York, on 8/1/1917, was an assistant general from 1964 to 1970.

She faithfully wrote Reverend Mother Rainsford[19] and the Eden Hall community. Her letters are vibrant and exuded life. Upon her arrival in Rome, on February 21, 1966, she detailed her experience:

> Since Saturday, I have been hoping that the famous cablegram really did reach you intact. When the Alitalia agent at the airport heard that I wanted to send a safe arrival cable, he told me that Alitalia would do it, free of charge, through their own network—so I put my trust in God and his cheerful disposition—and said "Gracia!" (or something like that with great gusto!)

She continued her letter describing the wheelchair that awaited her upon her arrival in Rome.

> Incidentally, there was a wheelchair waiting for me at the foot of the plane steps and so—Kaplunk!—in I went, while *all* other passengers were herded into the Roman version of a go-cart and off to customs, while I was pushed by my puffing Italian chauffeur up the long, two-story ramp, and then the entire length of the terminal. He trotted and maneuvered me like a Fiat through the heart of Rome at rush hour. No casualties! Of *all* the bags we had, the customs inspector thought only one suspicious and worth questioning—the one wrapped in brown paper.
>
> We reached the Mother House just before noon and were warmly welcomed as the first arrivals, by Reverend Mother Meliá[20] and the Community. Our Mother General[21] was out, so we did not meet her.
>
> Shortly thereafter (after dinner), we were whisked off to bed. The others went to an early evening Mass at St. Agnes, but since Reverend Mother thought it best for me to remain in bed—I stayed there, had supper (brought by the infirmarian and Reverend Mother herself)—went back to sleep and got up Sunday morning. I felt fine!

[19] Virginia Rainsford, RSCJ, born in Philadelphia on 9/6/1908, was a superior in the Washington Province. She died on 12/27/1997 in Albany, New York.
[20] Magdalena Melia, RSCJ, was born 6/6/1904, in Puerto Rico. She was assistant general and in charge of the probation during the 1960s. She died in Santurce, Puerto Rico, 7/23/1988.
[21] The superior general was Sabine de Valon.

Our Mother (for these two weeks) goes out every day, morning and afternoon, to meet with the International Union of Superiors General—for a workshop, so she is not even here for meals. The Committee, of which she was previously President, is now really going to be active, and she thinks it is capable of great good. She is one of five (I think) Counselors [*sic*].[22] Among others who have come to participate is Sister Luke[23] from Loretto Heights. Reaction to her here is much the same as in the United States... very interesting...extraordinary...etc. And Our Mother was "happy to meet her."

Not all the Probanists have arrived. The entire Spanish contingent is expected at 11:00 this evening. Srs. Peña and Martínez have not yet been able to wrest visas from Fidel[24], so...we await news! The two from Cuba who are waiting on visas.... There are no French, one Italian, and two Brazilians. These latter brought two Brazilian postulants who are to enter at Frascati! We also have in the Probation, Sr. Helen McLaughlin,[25] the Scottish aspirant, who has been missionary to Uganda for the past year.

Père Bernard will give us two classes a week! One in Scripture, and the other on something concerning *Perfectae Caritatis*![26] I have not met him, but all say that he is truly a "man of God." He will give the Mistresses of Novices a conference in the morning and have a "round table" in the afternoon.

Please thank everyone in the Community for me once again—for all that they did for me. How I *loved* the miniature trousseau—I had a wonderful time "unpacking" each thing. I count very, very much on those prayers and offerings, that God will find room to "work" in me—or rather that I will let Him!

[22] At the beginning of the third session of Vatican II in 1964 and 1965, the Pope appointed women auditors. Because of her earlier role in the founding of UISG, Mother de Valon was named one of them for the third and fourth sessions.

[23] Sister Mary Luke Tobin, SL., former superior general of the Sisters of Loretto and president of LCWR, was also an auditor at the Second Vatican Council.

[24] Kit is misinformed here; these two Cubans were not coming from Cuba; there were no RSCJ there at the time.

[25] Helen McLaughlin, RSCJ, a Scot, served in Uganda and later as superior general, 1982-1994.

[26] The title of the Vatican Council's decree on religious life.

You, Reverend Mother, know how much I want to be
open, available, present to Him—and *authentic*. "Yes, Lord
at every moment and in every situation." Thank you, again,
with all my heart. I join you strongly in your prayers for
me—the tag of the trousseau!

The next day, she wrote:

We had our Mother's conference for the opening of
Probation this afternoon. It was on "Perfectae Caritatis—
Perfect Charity," as the theological foundation for religious
life. While Religious have the same obligation as all
baptized—the difference is in our seeking *perfect charity*—
perfection by total consecration—in existing *seriously* and
exclusively for God. It was beautiful and thanks be to God,
I could understand her French *perfectly*. I could not get over
how strongly and *intensely* she speaks. Her voice completes
the meaning of the words she uses—sooo powerful!

Please give my love to Reverend Mother Tobin when
she comes. I am to be her secretary when she returns. Isn't
that great!!

I pray much for you. Please bless your loving and
grateful child in C.J.M.

Kit Collins, R.S.C.J."

The numerous and lengthy letters Kit wrote to her parents from
Rome demonstrate her love for them. She wrote as often as she was
allowed, detailing her everyday life in Rome, relating humorous incidents,
and ruminating on the desire to live solely for God, manifesting perfect
charity for all. In a letter written in March, Kit describes life in Rome
specially tailored for her parents:

The weather has been wonderful *looking*. It is nice and sunny,
but sooo cold. They keep saying that this is spring, but I am
happy with all my woolies. They call me "granny" of the
Probation. I wear woolies and take the elevator. But I feel
fine—while they sniffle. (We have some good laughs over it.)

Several of the nuns brought with them pictures and
slides of the noviceships in their respective countries, so we
have three nights worth of really interesting viewing. It is
wonderful and consoling to see evidence of the tremendous
unity throughout the Society, regardless of country, and

the circumstances, and customs of each nation and people. Speaking of pictures, the Polaroid has made a great hit.

In another note to her parents, she commented on the St. Patrick's Day card they sent her. It is worth noting the importance of St. Patrick's Day in her life as an Irish Catholic in the United States.

> Thank you for the St. Pat's Day card. I put it in my pocket. When I get into the elevator—and when I bumped against the side, it gives out a big squawk—gives my companion a start and us a good chuckle. The Irish Probanists were wearing the green, as we all went down after supper for a little of "When Irish Eyes Are Smiling" and McNamara's band—Indians, Spanish, and Congolese singing for all they were worth…. It is wonderful to have the opportunity to talk with people who have a real common bond, and yet who have such different cultures, ideas, customs, etc. We get a good amount of time for dialog in all kinds of things. It is enriching to say the least.

Because of her heart attack at an early age, her health was a concern to her and to others, so she continued:

> I am feeling perfectly fine and they are giving me royal care—much more cautious than I would be. At this rate, by July, I will not only be strong, I'll be a veritable "Tarzan" (or Jane, I should say). I have no worry on that score.
> I pray for you very much; you may be certain of that. At Easter, there will be more news to report, so I shall write again then. Stay your good selves. Much love, in C.J.M.
> Kit Collins, RSCJ

In April that year, Kit wrote a famous letter to her parents in which she used the image of a crocodile and an elephant to describe the mission of the Society, which, uniquely, captured her apostolic zeal. She began by telling them about the Easter Vigil: "I stayed up for the Easter Vigil, which began at 11:00 and ended about 1:30—so I have become a 'night owl' once again."

Then followed a description of a gathering of the probanists about Uganda:

For the viewing, I was plucked down beside Mother McLaughlin, a Scot who has been on the mission there. Consequently, I learned a few extra practical points. For example, if you are being chased by a crocodile (and they run fast always "mouth open") run zigzag, and you will be all right. They can't turn their hungry little bodies very quickly. Also if you meet up with an elephant, check the direction of the wind. If you can smell him, that's fine (well, at least it is safe), but if you're on the wrong side, and if he smells human meat, it's curtains! So, the idea is, if you want to be a good missionary—run zig zag and stay on the right side of the elephant."

It was a life lesson Kit took to heart. She was certainly a visionary, a missionary who charted new courses throughout her life. She ran zigzag and navigated on the right side of the elephant!

On June 24, 1966, she wrote of her audience with Pope Paul VI:

Did you hear that I had the good fortune to see the Holy Father on June 3rd? Reverend Mother Tobin got tickets for us for the great Solemn Anniversary Requiem for John XXIII. We went with Reverend Mother on the bus, no less, right in the midst of campaigning going on for the Italian elections, which was an education in itself! Italians politics is really something—13 parties in the running—all driving around town with huge signs…. One of the little "pressures" was games like calling a mail strike—so far, days practically no inter-city mail, and very little air mail. They said that bags were piled high at the airport (something like 20 million letters). I think they're being casual about this kind of thing, so that when the strike is on, some were sorted and delivered, some sorted and dumped….

Kathleen Conan,[27] the Society's superior general from 2008 to 2016, recalled a story of Kit in probation:

[27] Kathleen Conan, RSCJ, an American, born in Syracuse, New York, 4/15/1947, was provincial in the United States and then superior general, 2008-2016.

> I remember the story of the Mother House's elevator when Kit was in Probation. Because of her heart attack, Kit had permission to use the elevator. Wanting a companion, she would say to Meg Canty, "You get in with me."

Helen McLaughlin, superior general from 1982 to1994, worked with Kit at general chapters and named her chair of the International Education Commission (IEC). She also remembers the elevator in connection with Kit and gives a hint of Kit's irreverence toward authority figures:

> I first met Kit in February 1966, when we were in the same probation. At that time, we did not have many possibilities for conversing. What I remember about Kit is that given a health condition, she was not to climb up the stairs, but had to take the lift. We would see Meg [Canty] and Kit waiting together for the lift to come. Mère de Valon, superior general, also took the lift, and when she was delayed in the Ave Maria corner having a conversation with one of the community, I noticed that Kit and a companion walked as quickly as possible towards the lift and got into it before Mère de Valon arrived. Sometimes they were in a naughty mood, and they would keep the lift upstairs, and delay Mère de Valon's getting it. They could see her waiting below, while they were keeping the lift upstairs. It was done in a spirit of fun!

Kit's profession ceremony was July 20, 1966, with Father Kibbell, SJ, as the celebrant. Mother de Valon, as superior general, received the vows of the probanists. Kit's parents attended the profession, which took place in the chapel of the motherhouse in Rome. The beautiful ceremony was one of the first to use the vernacular for the Eucharistic celebration and offer communion under both species. These liturgical reforms had been sanctioned by Vatican II in 1963 in the Constitution on the Sacred Liturgy.

The name (focus) given to the probation was *Probation de la Confiante Obéissance,* Probation of Confident Obedience. Kit faithfully lived that obedience all her life, doing at times what she would not have chosen to do. The *devise* [motto] of the probation was, "In professing obedience, religious offer the full surrender of their own will as a sacrifice of themselves to God." Mother de Valon encouraged the probanists to

"stay your wonderful selves, your good selves." For Mother de Valon the only way to grow in holiness was to be who God created you to be; that would mean striving to live authentically as a Religious of the Sacred Heart.

Early Professed Life

Leaving Rome, Kit returned to Eden Hall in Philadelphia as director of studies. She served in this role for two years, 1966 to 1968. Vicky Rajca, a student at the time, recalls Kit as a person who had an idea a minute.

During her time at Eden Hall, a Colombian religious, Emma Fernandez[28] came to know Kit. It was Kit's sense of humor, coupled with her kindness that impressed Emma. Kit took Emma under her wing to teach her English. Her first lesson was the Act of Contrition! When they met, Kit greeted Emma with, "Every day, every way, I am better and better," indicating that Emma was growing in grace and in the ability to speak English! It was Kit's way of encouraging her to continue to perfect her English.

Emma recalls that Kit was fun to be with, and she always thought of the community. At Eden Hall, Kit hosted candlelight suppers and candlelight dessert parties held in a room other than the refectory [the nuns' dining room]. "Kit was joyful and friendly, a wonderful community person. She included everyone, and everyone liked to be with her. She was very energetic, so much so that there were times Kit could not sleep." What Emma loved most about Kit was her humor and her expansive personality, which welcomed everyone to join her on the journey of life.

After both left Eden Hall, Emma and Kit would meet periodically at jubilees, funerals, or fusion days, days when RSCJ from different communities came together for recreation. Emma recalled that Kit always had a camera and acted as the photographer at such events.

[28] Emma Fernández, RSCJ, born in Bogotá, Colombia, on 4/5/1929, lived in many houses of the Washington Province.

Headmistress of Stone Ridge

In 1968, Kit was named mistress general [headmistress] of Stone Ridge Country Day School of the Sacred Heart in Bethesda, Maryland. Her four years there were marked by innovation and change, both in the curriculum and the extra-curricular activities of the school. She was forward thinking and pushed the faculty to move beyond the traditional boundaries of pedagogic methodology into unchartered realms of teaching

Kit had a gift of hiring creative people like herself to assist her in the mission of Sacred Heart education. One such educator was Vernon Dolphin. He was creative and imaginative and left his mark on the students at Stone Ridge. Their dynamic combination influenced the way students learned, as well as the way the faculty taught. Under Kit's leadership, Vernon Dolphin transformed the student council into what was named School Community Governance (SCG). SCG included all students, administration, faculty, and staff in the school. Betsy Hartson, who worked with Vernon and Kit, remembers, "The SCG worked with the broad picture, community and governance, and the responsibility was to reach and support everyone in the school." Fifty years later Stephany Fontanone, the upper school dean of students in 2017, described school governance at Stone Ridge:

> Stone Ridge is inseparable from the community of students, teachers, and parents that form the school. Governance is the mechanism through which a community can make known its interests and goals. The school community governance program allows students to have a forum for bringing important community interests to the consciousness of the entire school. A community governance structure allows students to take a share of leadership and be involved in activities of their own design based on student interests. The principles of the program are knowledge, distribution

of responsibility, self-government, skill development, community, and self-expression."

It is a testimony to Kit's and Vernon Dolphin's leadership that this inclusive model of governance was operative for years and has only now been modified to meet the needs of the time.

Another program introduced by Dolphin and sanctioned by Kit was the Middle School Lab, a creative activity in which students worked in groups around tables rather than in a traditional classroom structure. Again, the emphasis was on inclusion and collaboration, work Kit valued highly as a way for students to learn. Betsy Hartson noted, "Both programs were unique and expressed Society values and new approaches at Stone Ridge." And both were examples of Kit's futurist thinking and vision of education.

Sharon Collins,[29] middle school head several years later, still recalls some solid advice that Kit gave her:

> I also remember, when we were living together at Stone Ridge, and I was new middle school head, and very nervous about a meeting with a board member/parent who was on the warpath, that Kit gave me the simple, but solid advice to say very little and, with a serious attitude, to take lengthy notes. This proved an elegant tactic and one that I have passed on to many colleagues over the years.

Sharon continues:

> Her strengths were, in my opinion, her love of ideas, of process and of communicating. She did not like mundane details and was easily bored. The one weakness I noted in Kit was that she really loved people, but would prioritize her attention to those who were more important. This was not that she was uncaring or snobbish, but rather, I think, that influence was a strong drive in her. She was an amazing woman—so vibrant and creative. As an educator and an administrator, Kit made life happen. She was not content to leave things as they were or with the status quo. She reached for new heights and brought the faculty and staff with her.

[29] Sharon Collins, former RSCJ, born in Brooklyn, New York, on 4/13/1947. She taught at Stone Ridge, Atherton, and other Network schools.

As Kit's "fair-haired child," Vernon had license to innovate, but also became a lightning rod for criticism. Some of his techniques and methods were controversial, alienating faculty, parents, and students. For example, he build a yurt, a circular Scandinavian dwelling with a hole in the center, at the back of the campus where he held his classes. He encouraged faculty to do the same.

Sandy Theunick,[30] former RSCJ, who worked as dean of students at Stone Ridge for six years, said that Kit, immediately "took me under her wing." Sandy remembers those years as being educationally progressive and visionary. Sandy first met Kit at a fusion day, although she heard of her before that. "Margaret Mary Coakley,[31] mistress of novices, had spoken of Kit to us in the noviceship when Kit as a young nun had had a heart attack," she said. In fact, they met at Eden Hall. "We were friends then and remained friends. Kit always accepted me as I was." Sandy describes Kit as being always on the cutting edge, a characteristic that made her stand out and, at the same time, separated her. She was a genius, but that gift brought isolation and vulnerability to her life. Sandy pointed out that Kit had many good friends in the U.S. and around the world. Often, Kit would stay up at night with her friends discussing the day's issues. Sandy remembered: "We stayed up late solving the problems of the world."

Mary Helen McComas[32] commented: "Tensions were high at Stone Ridge during Kit's short tenure. There were too many changes in such a small space of time." The times were tumultuous, as were the circumstances at Stone Ridge. Although a creative and futurist thinker, Kit left chaos in her wake. Anne Dyer,[33] lower school head at the time, described the situation as "slash and burn," in which life went from bad to worse. Reverend Mother Bultó, the superior general of the Society, arrived with her assistant, Reverend Mother Mary Elizabeth

[30] Sandra Theunick, former RSCJ and colleague of Kit's, was born in Pontiac, Michigan, on 6/1/1946; she stayed in contact with Kit.

[31] Margaret Mary "Mavie" Coakley, RSCJ, born in Cleveland, Ohio, on 4/11/1920, was mistress of novices from 1959 to 1967 and later worked in New York at Encore Community Services, an eldercare organization. She died on 7/2/2011.

[32] Mary Helen McComas, RSCJ, born in Baltimore, 5/21/1933, was business manager in Network schools and served in the finance office at the motherhouse.

[33] Anne Dyer, RSCJ, born in Washington, D.C., on 8/11/1937, worked with Kit at Stone Ridge, where she was later headmistress.

Tobin, in the course of an official visit to the United States. At the community meeting, no one talked, so Reverend Mother Bultó called another meeting. It was clear that tensions were high in the community. Soon after, Kit was sent to Greenwich. Although it was obvious that Kit's sudden departure was the direct result of her own actions, Kit had never let anyone know she was overwhelmed. Kit was creative, innovative, and brilliant, but at times she was not collaborative and did not share her needs readily. The minutes of the meeting of the Washington Province Council, March 2, 1971, record in part:

> It seems best that Sister Sweeney [Provincial of the Washington Province] should tell Kit Collins definitely that she wants Kit to be education director of the Province and wants her to live in Newton—to work in the Provincial House but to live in a community. The Council agreed that Kit Collins should be Education Director and not Headmistress at Stone Ridge."

In a letter to the Washington Province on March 30, 1971, Sister Elizabeth Sweeney wrote:

> Sister Catherine Collins has agreed to serve as Educational Director of the Washington Province. This will, of course, entail her leaving her position as Headmistress at Stone Ridge.... Sister Collins's work will take her round the Province, but she will reside in Boston when she is not traveling. Because of the interprovincial educational cooperation, Sister Collins herself will be in touch with you concerning your expectations of how she can best serve the interests of each school and the college in the overall working of the province. The office of Education Director has been well documented ever since the first recommendations of the Planning Commission, and later, in the Provincial Chapter documents of last year. There is little that I can add to this, except to say that I depend very much on Sister Collins to assist me, and all of us, in planning and decision-making for the future educational endeavors of this Province. Sister Collins will begin her work full-time as Education Director this summer.

Ann Taylor, a member of the Stone Ridge community at the time, remembers: "Kit was exhausted. The school was wearing her out. Kit had been named to a new position. So after spring break it was decided that she leave Stone Ridge before the end of the school year." Clare McGowan[34] assumed her duties.

Despite the abrupt end of her tenure, Kit had brought the school into the twentieth century. In the short two-and-a-half years she was there, Kit freed students and faculty to broaden their vision and think in new ways. She had the courage of her convictions and fearlessly moved ahead. Some called this trait "stubbornness," others called it "courage." Convinced she was right, Kit forged ahead, sometimes oblivious to the feelings of people around her. Kit was convinced that, from one point of view, Sacred Heart schools were businesses and the faculty must be professionals. This description was a new way of viewing Sacred Heart schools and became a challenge for all administrators.

In 1971, when Kit was appointed director of education for the Washington Province, the province included the following schools: Stone Ridge in Bethesda, Portsmouth in Rhode Island, Newton Academy and Newton College in Newton, Massachusetts, Stuart in Princeton, New Jersey, and Carrollton in Miami, Florida. When Kit assumed this position, there was no written job description. This lack, however, did not stop Kit from taking the reins and moving forward. She was staff to the provincial, Sister Elizabeth Sweeney[35] and her team. On her team was Sandy Theunick, former dean of students at Stone Ridge. Sandy saw Kit as needing and seeking approval. "Although Kit was very accomplished, she would struggle with acceptance and belonging issues all her life. She cleverly hid her neediness from most."

Mary Jane Ferrier lived with Kit in Boston in the early 1970s. Although they were doing different works, they would meet at the end of the day and share stories. "Kit was a great storyteller!" She was a big thinker who "didn't suffer fools gladly." She also loved to relax. Mary Jane recalls that Kit loved to go to the races and enjoyed playing bridge. If Kit was late coming home, "Hearing her car turn into the

[34] Clare McGowan, RSCJ, was born in Watertown, Massachusetts, on 8/1/1927. She served as headmistress in Miami and at Stone Ridge for many years. She died in Atherton, California, on 11/9/1993.

[35] Elizabeth Sweeney, RSCJ, was born in Rochester, New York, on 12/13/1914. After many years as superior in the houses of the Washington Province, she was named provincial. She died in Albany on 11/26/2008.

driveway, we would race upstairs to bed, for we knew if we stayed, we would be there for hours." Although outwardly flamboyant, Kit was a very private person. As Mary Jane Ferrier observed: "She was an Irish Catholic, close to Christ, but she did not talk about her spiritual life, and she also kept her hurts to herself, or would laugh at them."

Kathleen Conan reflected upon Kit's worldview.

> Kit's world was big, and she kept expanding it. She included family, RSCJ, and lay people—men and women. She had the ability to "draw people out" and bring them along! The Network, which she started, was about connections. Kit was loyal to these connections. Her long-time friends met faithfully once a year and shared life. Ronnie Dewey, Mickey McKay, Nance O'Neil, and Kit were faithful to each other, and their bonds ran deep.

At times, her boisterous demeanor covered her warmth, but Kathy insisted that Kit was, above all, tender and reflective. Her heart was wide and warm, and her close friends and acquaintances attest to that. She continually connected people.

Origins of the Network

Kit served as the Washington Province director of education for only a year, 1971-1972. Her life took an unexpected turn when she was asked by the Interprovincial Board (the provincials of the then five provinces in the United States) to be the National Coordinator for Sacred Heart Schools in the U.S.A. Saying yes changed her life and reset the course of Sacred Heart education in the U.S.—and eventually around the world.

The idea of a network—a union of Sacred Heart schools—had begun to be formulated and discussed. East coast schools, because of their proximity to one another, saw the advantages of such an arrangement for sharing resources, curricula, and perhaps, personnel. The heads of the eastern schools asked Joan Kirby,[36] headmistress of the Convent of the Sacred Heart, 91st Street in New York City, to be their spokesperson and write to the Interprovincial Board to request the establishment of a network. On July 25, 1972, Joan Kirby wrote to Sister Margaret Mary Coakley, provincial of the New York Province. In this letter, the heads of school suggested an educational coordinator be named to the staff of the Interprovincial Board:

> She need not be full time, but should have enough time to concentrate on the network of schools. Instead of "apostolic coordinator," she might be called "coordinator of schools" or "executive secretary for the schools." Her job description would have to be clearly defined.

[36] Joan Kirby, RSCJ, born in New York on 5/24/1926, was headmistress at 91st Street in New York, from 1969 to 1981. Later she became executive director of the Temple of Understanding, an NGO, the oldest interfaith organization affiliated with the UN. She died 9/9/2015.

We feel that there is a person, not only eminently talented for this kind of task, but also now doing it for the Washington Province: Sr. Catherine Collins. Could she perform this service for the whole country? If she could continue to make Boston her base of activity, then she would be near Sr. Jean Ford,[37] chairman [sic] of the IPB and Sr. Ann Conroy,[38] as well, who has already had many contacts with the schools of the country. We would hope that the latter would have time to help Sr. Collins and would be able to enlist the interest of the novices in the work of the network of schools.

Thus, the idea of the Network of Sacred Heart Schools was presented to Sister Coakley—an idea, as Joan Kirby aptly put it, "which we think to be of considerable importance!"

The idea of a network of schools was presented to the Interprovincial Board at its meeting in St. Louis in the summer of 1972. The 1960s in the United States had been marked by sweeping changes in Sacred Heart educational institutions. The number of elementary and secondary schools decreased between 1968 and 1975. Each province had hired a management consulting firm to advise in its decision-making. These commissions were composed of representative RSCJ and consultants from two firms. Following the recommendations of the commissions, each of the provinces closed one or more schools. These closings were based in part on demographics, on deferred maintenance of some of the buildings, on a reduction in the number of available religious teachers and administrators, and a lack of vision regarding collaboration with the laity. Fewer women were entering religious life and many women were leaving. Many religious were electing to work in ministries other than the schools. With the decline of the number of religious in the schools and concurrently the development of independent boards of trustees responsible for specific schools, the need for the Society of the Sacred Heart to safeguard its philosophy and historical tradition became increasingly clear to Sacred Heart educators, lay and religious

[37] Jean Ford, born in Boston, 5/19/1926, was a teacher and administrator in Network schools for many years before becoming successively provincial of the Washington Province and assistant general of the Society, 1988-1994. She died in Albany, New York, 5/16/2012.

[38] Ann Conroy, RSCJ, born in Belle Harbor, New York, on 7/9/1925. At the time in question, she was director of novices. Subsequently, she was the last provincial of the New York Province. She died at Oakwood on 8/5/2016.

alike. A national coordinator could strengthen a network, expand its influence, and ultimately provide an education beyond academic proficiency to a value-based philosophy that fostered the individual worth of students and a sense of community.

As Kit Collins seemed, indeed, the ideal person to form such a network and then to lead it forward, the Interprovincial Board of the five U.S. Provinces asked her to be the first National Coordinator of Sacred Heart schools. They saw her as a strategic leader with proven organization and communication skills, as well as a visionary educator and administrator with a great sense of humor. Kit was the ideal person for the next ten years. Kit accepted this ministry to create and lead the Network at a time when there was much healing to be done following the turbulent years of school closings and the relocating of many Religious of the Sacred Heart.

In the wake of this pain and disillusionment with the Society, the five provincials who followed, Ann Conroy, Clare Pratt[39], Rosemary Dewey, Rita Karam,[40] and Rita Maginn,[41] endeavored to find a new way to operate Sacred Heart schools in the absence of religious. They sought to respect established, long-term relationships. They saw that to achieve this end, a strategic collaboration had to be formed between the religious and the laypersons who worked in the Sacred Heart schools. The formation of the Network was the means settled on with Kit Collins as the person to implement it in her role as national coordinator.

True to her core beliefs, Kit knew that she could not—and did not want to—develop goals for this new organization and its evaluation process by herself. She wanted to model from the beginning how this collaborative structure would work. So, she gathered a group of educators from across the country, one from each province, which she called The School Committee. They provided input from the educators of all five provinces

In addition as National Coordinator for Sacred Heart Schools, one of Kit's first initiatives was the creation of the Stuart Conferences.

[39] Clare Pratt, RSCJ, born in Washington, D.C., on 11/23/1939, was provincial of the Washington Province. She later became secretary general, then superior general of the Society of the Sacred Heart, 2000-2008.

[40] Rita Karam, RSCJ, was born in Kinder, Louisiana, on 4/13/1929. She was provincial of the St. Louis Province, and later assistant general. She died in New Orleans on 11/14/1996.

[41] Rita Maginn, RSCJ, born in Red Oak, Iowa, on 8/13/1926, was provincial of the California Province. She died at Oakwood on 11/25/1991.

Named after one of the great educators of the Society, Mother Janet Stuart, these gatherings, held at Maryville in St. Louis in the summer of 1971 and in Cleveland in summer 1974, brought educators from each of the then nineteen schools in the United States together for an educational meeting. Both conferences provided a forum where they could come together as Sacred Heart educators to discuss educational philosophy, ideas and successes, examine challenges, explore new paths, and forge new relationships not bound by school or city.

In the keynote address at the Stuart Conference in Cleveland, in the summer of 1974, Kit reflected upon the essence of Sacred Heart education:

> ...We are gathered here, I believe, and I believe this, truly for a special reason. We've come not merely to share information, because we could do that elsewhere, and in other ways; and not only to hear people speak about education, excellent though they might be. So we are here bound by a philosophy of education—inarticulate as it may sometimes be—and by religious conviction, to share both the hope and the work of renewing our vision of Sacred Heart Education and of working together toward very concrete ways of living that out ever more truly.[42]

Kit knew that these educators would achieve educational excellence in their particular locations and would collaborate with other independent and Catholic administrators and teachers; but when they gathered in Cleveland, Kit wanted them to see themselves as Sacred Heart educators first, accountable to one another as they moved forward. Kit told them they were together "to clarify, to identify, and to articulate, what it really means to be a Sacred Heart school, and what being Sacred Heart educators really means. That, I believe, is a life-long struggle, and I hope it will never be otherwise."

The Stuart Conference in Cleveland included the first significant lay participation in the formation of the Network. At this meeting, participants grappled with questions such as "What makes a Sacred Heart School?" and "What did membership in the Network mean, and what were the requirements for membership?" This group worked with

[42] All quotations from Kit Collins's talks and writings are in the Archives of the United States – Canada Province of the Society of the Sacred Heart, St. Louis, Missouri.

developed models ranging from the McDonald's franchise model to a highly centralized national school board. Participants realized the need for criteria, for standards against which a school could measure itself as a Sacred Heart school and for which they could be held accountable to the Interprovincial Board of Provincials (IPB). Following this meeting, the School Committee was asked to manage a process that would ensure as much involvement as possible of constituents within the schools in answering the question, "What makes a school a Sacred Heart school?" These men and women knew that the description of what makes a school "Sacred Heart" would not necessarily include the presence of many nuns nor would it include the preservation of many of the customs and traditions that had marked Sacred Heart schools in the past. The conference was meant specifically to examine with other Sacred Heart educators the essence of this unique education. Kit's address continued:

> I think there are some things we can look to for reflection, and hopefully for enlightenment. The first of those, and perhaps the most obvious, is that which we draw from the history and the tradition of Sacred Heart schools, best expressed perhaps in what we have called historically, the "Plan of Studies," which is really an incredible document, which was frequently and seriously updated from 1805 until 1958. So we can see a genuine evolution in our thinking and in our sense about the meaning of Sacred Heart education.

Looking back at the history of Sacred Heart education, Kit summarized it in one word:

> And if I were to choose one word that I thought really captured the spirit of our past, I think I would choose the word *integrity*, in its deepest and perhaps even, its scriptural sense. It describes basically, I think, the character of our education.

Then she turned to the future:

> I think the other thing we have to look to is what it means to be a Sacred Heart educator. And we have sources for this challenge, I believe, which are etymological, theological, and symbolic. To be an educator means, in its deepest sense,

to lead forth, to call forth, to bring up, to raise, in fact, to be mother. And that does not mean male or female to be mother.

In this keynote, Kit told the educators gathered in Cleveland the purpose of the meeting: She wanted them to spend time as Sacred Heart educators:

> ...to reflect together, to plan together, to build together, and to hope together, seriously, because our times demand it of us, and enthusiastically, because our faith asks it of us. And I make a note that the word 'enthusiasm' comes from the Greek '*en/theos*' (God within; God inspired). That is the kind of enthusiasm that we have to draw on and that our faith asks of us too, at this time. And if we allow ourselves to be confronted by those two powerful, haunting phrases: 'obstruction of justice' and 'misuse of power,' as we meet here these days, our response should be, and I think, must be, to seek, to work in our schools for the establishment of justice, and the purification of power, and to do so in the double context of: who we are, and what the structures of learning are that we create.

For her, this meant that students should be educated to integrity and justice. "That is awesome," she said, "and I think it is tremendously exciting." She continued,

> So, I have drawn up some questions here that suggest the kinds of things we might ask ourselves together:
>
> 1) Is the individual student cherished as unique—and do we demand, compassionately, nothing short of his or her full growth?
>
> 2) Is that fullness and growth sought—not at the expense of others—but for their good?
>
> 3) Do structures within and without the classroom foster integration, integrity; do they say that healthy, mutual interdependence is important; that students can learn together and from one another?

4) Are students educated in leadership—not handed positions of responsibility for which they are ill prepared and bound to fail; but are they educated to decision making with real responsibility? Where are students structurally located in the school?

Kit stressed that Sacred Heart educators teach by who they are as opposed to what they say, "which is at the very center of our effectiveness as Sacred Heart educators." In the last analysis, she said, "we educate and are educated by structures we pattern and who we are." She concluded her keynote:

> Calling the assembly to become increasingly what we mean by Sacred Heart educators, we have to come face to face with the profound realities of the world in which we live— or better, the world which is OURS. We need to be true to our word and faithful to our vision. True to our word in envisioning the word we speak: the word of truth, integrity, of justice. The word of the power of love, of compassion, and to be faithful to our vision—and I do believe that together we have a great hope and a great vision. We even have, in the best sense, great power. "The just man justices," Hopkins says. To be faithful to that vision, we ourselves have to be faithful; for that, I believe, is the source of our life, our wholeness, and our justice.

Kit ended with one of her favorite quotes from Alfred Tennyson's "Ulysses," calling those gathered to seek a better world, to create a new reality through education:

> ... Come, my friends
> 'Tis not too late to seek a newer world.
> Push off, and sitting well in order smite
> The sounding furrows; for my purpose holds
> To sail beyond the sunset, and the baths
> Of all the Western stars, until I die.
> * * * * *
> Though much is taken, much abides; and though
> We are not now that strength which in old days
> Moved earth and heaven; that which we are, we are,
> One equal temper of heroic hearts,
> Made weak by time and fate, but strong in will

To strive, to seek, to find, and not to yield.

Subsequently, smaller, interest-based meetings proved more beneficial and served the needs of the educators better than national meetings. But these two Stuart Conferences set the stage for the Network, because the attendees for the first time saw "the Network." They met, dialogued, and learned from one another. In other words, they experienced "the Network" and were energized and enriched by one another.

In 1970, the Society of the Sacred Heart held a general chapter, the highest governing body of the Society. It was the second chapter after the close of Vatican II, and, as such, it was pivotal in setting a new direction for the Society. It affirmed that the mission of the Society was education: "At a time when the integral development of man [sic] is a task of special urgency, we reaffirm our educational mission as our service in the Church." Turning to the future, the chapter urged the Society to bring all its creativity to bear on this mission. In light of this mission, the 1970 chapter called the Society to focus especially on the young. "It is the love of Christ which urges us to meet the needs of those weighed down by ignorance or servitude, and above all, the needs of the young who search for meaning in their life."

Calling on the members of the Society to bring their creativity to the educational mission, the chapter asked the Society to: "educate to a faith which will be relevant in a secularized world, to a deep respect for intellectual values, and to a social awareness which will impel to action." These words would be used almost verbatim in 1975 in the articulation of what were named Goals and Criteria for Sacred Heart Schools in the United States.

The section from the 1970 chapter on the Society's educational mission in the Church concludes with a desire to scrutinize the apostolic value of various institutions of the Society. "In this perspective, we wish to examine seriously the apostolic value of our institutions and to take appropriate action." With this mandate, Kit began to think not about individual schools, but about a Network of Sacred Heart schools. She envisioned Sacred Heart schools united by core values, but distinct in their operations.

Goals and Criteria

Guided by her core belief that more can be achieved together than separately, Kit knew that common goals were needed to connect the then nineteen schools of the Sacred Heart across the country. Broad enough to touch each school, the goals also had to express the essence of Sacred Heart schools. What better place to begin than with the Chapter of 1970, which had just recently re-articulated the educational mission of the Society in what the Chapter called "options." The first three goals of Sacred Heart education, taken directly from the 1970 Chapter are:

- a faith which is relevant in a secularized world;
- a deep respect for intellectual values, and
- a social awareness which impels action.

Two more goals express key elements of Sacred Heart education: the building of community as a Christian value and personal growth in an atmosphere of wise freedom. These last two goals were a hallmark of Sacred Heart education from its inception by Saint Madeleine Sophie Barat. All five goals together express the essence of the education given at a Sacred Heart school.

Bill Gallop,[43] headmaster of the Academy of the Sacred Heart in New Orleans from 1973 to 1984, was a member of the group Kit formed to write the *Goals and Criteria* for schools. Bill noted that it took this committee four years to interview faculty and staff, visit with administrators, and talk with school constituents in all Sacred Heart schools in this country in order to form the "non-negotiable" tenets of Sacred Heart education. The result was the five Goals, based on the 1970 statements of the Society, as we have seen: faith, intellectual life,

[43] Bill Gallop was a long time Network educator who subsequently founded in New Orleans a school for boys named after Janet Erskine Stuart.

social justice, community and personal growth. When the committee visited the various schools, their focus was always, "What is your mainstay here at...," "What is the essence of your 'Sacred Heartness?'"

According to Bill Gallop, Kit, of course, was the inspiration behind this project. "The word became flesh in Kit," Gallop asserted. She was the inspiration, the charismatic leader, who used her imagination to lead the group! The group also worked with a consultant, David Ruhmkorff,[44] who insisted on the articulation of a mission statement. Bill Gallop stated, "With David Ruhmkorff's input, we accepted the 'Franchise model'! There are many Sacred Heart schools, but each has its own unique identity. Our first task was to uncover non-negotiables of Sacred Heart education. This took three to four years of visiting all the Network schools. Then a year or more of articulating these into goal statements, and then reviewing the comments from all heads." The writing of Goals and Criteria was a collaborative process, involving the whole of the Network, from the start.

Judy Garson,[45] another member of the committee, remembers Kit's early insight that, down the road, there would not be enough RSCJ to administer all the schools. Therefore, she insisted they not count on the presence of the religious to ensure that the schools would be truly "of the Sacred Heart." There had to be a process that moved the schools from generalizations to practical indicators. The five overarching goals with criteria that could be measured became the standards for the schools. Judy reflected:

> Kit (Washington Province) chaired the committee, and there were representatives of each province. George Bryant was Chicago, Bill Gallop was the South (New Orleans), I was New York, and Rita Maginn, California. It's interesting that there were (at least) two laypeople—and men besides— on the committee!
>
> We did the last draft in Boston. We were struggling with the Preamble, and eventually I had the sense that things were coming together. So they let me go off for a half-hour

[44] David Ruhmkorff was an educational consultant who worked with the Network. He died in 2007.

[45] Judith Garson, RSCJ, born in New York City on 4/11/1936, was at this point involved in the Network schools; later, she was assistant general, and after returning to New York, directed a multi-service community center in Harlem.

and write something that worked. It was not the whole Preamble, it was the seventh paragraph that begins:

"It is never safe, however, to assume too much. Values taken for granted or left unarticulated can become inoperative. Patterns of leadership and governance, the make-up of faculties and student bodies have changed rapidly, and as the schools of the Sacred Heart enter the mainstream of American independent education, they feel its characteristic pressures and strains. As they become increasingly diverse, it becomes increasingly necessary to respond to the question: "What makes a Sacred Heart school?" Independent but never isolated, every Sacred Heart school needs to feel the strength of belonging to a larger whole, of sharing principles and values, broad purposes, hopes and ambitions."

Of course, the whole thing has been re-worked countless times since then, but it has certainly stood the test of time.

Approved by the five provincials of the U.S. in 1975, the *Goals* became the guiding principles, the vision, for the schools. Kit, however, knew that having the goals was not enough to ensure that a school was "Sacred Heart." There had to be a regular, uniform system of accountability. Each school in different regions of the U.S. would live the mission uniquely, but each school would be accountable to the provincial and her team every five years to demonstrate concretely that it was living the mission of the Society responsibly. To create such a process, Kit sought the advice and wisdom of Thomas Groome,[46] a professor of Theology and Religious Education at Boston College. He describes the process in his own words:

When I first came to teach at Boston College (1976), I was still in the priesthood (and would be for eight more years). Blessedly, I found myself in one of the best pastoral "assignments" I've ever had—as mass-priest to the RSCJ communities in the Newton area. I celebrated at least three times a week in various communities and the others would join us. This gave me an introduction to the rich RSCJ charism, and especially its commitment to quality education. As I became friends with sisters in the community, Sr.

[46] Thomas Groome, born in County Kildare, Ireland; a professor of theology at Boston College, he was a friend and colleague of Kit's.

Kit Collins emerged as one of the best. We both shared a passion for good education and for good religious education in particular.

At the time, I was coming off some intense experiences with Paulo Freire's work (e.g. in my dissertation) and figuring out how his insights might be appropriated into Catholic and religious education. As I shared my thoughts with Kit, she was most supportive and enthusiastic. Then she had the bright idea that what I had begun to call "a shared praxis approach" would be ideal for the task of evaluating schools—one of her responsibilities at the time.

Following Freire's principles, such a process would begin by inviting teachers and administrators to "name and reflect upon their own reality." In other words, rather than outsiders coming in to name it for them, the review committee would invite teachers and administrators to recognize what they are already doing well (always beginning with the positive), and then what they could be doing better—with why, what if, etc., questions. This involved essentially getting them to tell their own story and vision about the school.

Only having listened carefully to the reflections of the school's staff on their reality, then would the outside review people make suggestions or challenges from the RSCJ charism or from other positive sources and best practices for the school to consider to achieve a broader vision.

Then, to conclude, instead of "telling" the school and its staff what they should be doing going forward after the review, the closing move is to get them to come to see for themselves where they want and need to go, their next steps toward excellence, etc.

It is an alarmingly simple process but very different from a bunch of outsiders coming in to "tell a school what it's not doing well and how to do it better."

This commission (NCOG, later SHCOG)[47] and the process of accountability, with tested tweaks, is in place to this day. A timeline was created whereby each school was visited on a five-year cycle. At the beginning, every October, the schools to be visited met to be "trained" in the *Shared Praxis* method and the protocols important to the visit.

[47] National Commission on Goals, later Sacred Heart Commission on Goals.

Reflection was key, as Kathleen Conan said, "We kept reflecting! The essence of this process is its reflective nature."

The formation of the Network of Sacred Heart Schools in 1979 was a challenge that Kit's gifts matched. She had the analytical mind necessary to organize such an endeavor, the vision to see what components would be needed for it to function, to grow and change with the times. She designed, in collaboration with the School Committee, the structures that would support the Network then and in the years to come. Kit wrote[48]

> If the pursuit of excellence is part of a heritage (and I believe it is) then it means:

- The refusal to settle superficially;
- Holy dissatisfaction with incompletion;
- An unquenchable thirst for integrity;
- A rootedness in faith without which our lives have little meaning because the brokenness of our world is beyond our own power to heal and make whole.

She continues to describe Sacred Heart education:

> If that excellence is part of our heritage, it requires us, as Sacred Heart educators, to have a commitment because neither faith nor hope can be communicated by the disengaged but only by those with gracious confidence in the possibilities that we have before us. If we have the kind of commitment in life, it will ask a continual revision and redirection. Continual renewing of curriculum structures, the process of learning, the integrity of our own lives.

This was her manifesto about the education given in the Network of Sacred Heart Schools. For her, it began with the individual embracing the tenets of this education, not simply as a philosophy but as a way of life. This education was meant to shape the integrity of the lives of those who adopted its values.

Barbara Dawson,[49] who wore many hats in her dealings with Kit,

[48] Personal notes ARSH

[49] Barbara Dawson, RSCJ, born in San Francisco on 6/21/1948, has held many positions in the Society; she is the present superior general.

as director of ministry and later as provincial of the U.S. Province, reflected on Kit's contribution to education within the United States.

> I do think Kit was a visionary. Being part of creating the *Goals and Criteria* and later the Network, [she] changed the face of Sacred Heart education in the United States and beyond our borders. Kit was not the sole creator of the *Goals and Criteria*, but she took what was created by a small group and fanned the flame of mission in schools throughout the U.S. first and then in other countries. Kit really understood what it means to create a network and developed a dynamic and vibrant system. In the U.S., this Network of Sacred Heart Schools both built the body and established a way of mutual accountability through peer review as well as accountability to the Society. It laid the foundation for a wonderfully dynamic system of schools that bear our name and carry out what we are called to do in the twenty-first century.
>
> The *Goals and Criteria* have had a wide-reaching impact on Sacred Heart education.…. It is a powerful experience to walk into Sacred Heart schools both in the northern and southern hemispheres and see the Goals written in so many languages on so many walls, connected to so many cultures and realities. When I was in Taiwan, I was so touched to receive hundreds of little notes from elementary aged children explaining to me how the Goals make a difference in their lives. The fact that these goals have survived the test of time and still are the base of the ethos of Sacred Heart education speaks to their depth and to her understanding of how to inculcate the Society's long-term values into an educational system. We are reaping the benefits from her understanding that lay people can carry out the mission with the same passion and understanding as RSCJ.

Both Sisters Conan and Dawson cited the development of the Network, including the *Goals and Criteria*, and the evaluation process as Kit's major contributions to the U.S. Province and beyond to the international Society.

Early on at the training session attended by administrators and teachers in October 1979 at Barat College, Kit said that she "would like to talk about our Network, its place and its meaning [to us] as Sacred Heart educators and its covenanted expression articulated in the *Goals and Criteria.…*" She continued,

So I'd like now to focus on the *Goals and Criteria*, the expression for now of a beautiful tradition…a legacy…a heritage, but also as a vision and a commitment, an obligation from the past that presses us forward, expressed in the *Goals and Criteria*. And that's a vision, a commitment that is renewed continually by our membership, literally—men and women—who as Sacred Heart educators are linked to that tradition as to each other in their work as educators. So the *Goals and Criteria*, which are, in a sense, a condition of our membership, actually form the connectedness among us as a Network in the U.S. They represent what we hold in common, in very diverse settings, even within the United States, and you can look at the map—the map of the Network. The *Goals and Criteria* are the covenanted expression of our tending to the land. They also reflect the depth and strength, the breadth and the richness of a vision and commitment that span the globe today. So there's a timelessness to our tradition, and there's a timelessness to the expression of the demands of that tradition for today in our situation.

Kit concluded by placing the goals in a global perspective.

There are five things, at least, which we can say were always meant to characterize what we know as Sacred Heart education, regardless of time and place. In other words, those things which are hallmarks, that press us, whether we find ourselves in Ireland, in Africa, in Egypt, in Austria, or the United States…whether we find ourselves in any of those places from 1800 to 1979.

Her passion for the Goals and Criteria was evident, and she never missed an opportunity to convey this passion to other Sacred Heart educators. Kit wrote and delivered countless talks on what it means to be a Sacred Heart educator; some are typed, some in the form of notes in her own handwriting. In one set of handwritten notes, she describes what it means to be an educator: She says it is literally "to lead out of; to lead forth; to bring to life." She concludes that from within ourselves as Sacred Heart educators, and from the world in which we live, we hear this call to seek justice with the heart of an educator.

Society Seminar

Kit knew that the heart and soul of the school required well-trained teachers. A Sacred Heart school depended on faculty and administrators steeped in the tradition, heritage, and best practices of Sacred Heart education as well as best practices of teaching and school governance. To that end, Kit sought to establish a summer program for present and aspiring leaders of Sacred Heart schools. Summer, of course, was the ideal time for such an institute. Kit knew not only what would be needed for the program to be of value for the training of Sacred Heart educators, but she also wanted the program to be able to offer a degree.

To that end, Kit approached La Salle College run by the Christian Brothers in Philadelphia. In 1974, the college agreed to sponsor such a program if Kit, as Network coordinator, would establish and staff what was to be called *Society Seminars*. These seminars focused on the "Sacred Heartness" of the education provided in a Network school and gave guidance about being a leader in a school living the Goals and Criteria of Sacred Heart Schools. The participants attended Society Seminars and studied educational theory and methods, administrative protocol and best practices. The Society Seminar named the circumstances that formed the setting for the changes called for by Vatican II in terms that could be fully understood and assessed. Kit, always a loyal daughter of Saint Madeleine Sophie, was always at heart a teacher who sought clarity, knowledge, and understanding and wanted the same for those she instructed.

Perhaps, the popularity of the Society Seminars was that they provided a way to learn about the charism and mission of the Society and Sacred Heart education after Vatican II. The seminar program was established several years after the close of Vatican II, so the Society had had a number of years of experience of living religious life in a new way and of applying new insights to education. The educators

gathered at La Salle College wanted to know the mission well enough to pass it on to future educators in their respective schools. If Sacred Heart education was to continue, it would be through these people. The RSCJ and lay faculty and administrators needed to work as one to continue the mission.

In the summer of 1975, thirty-two educators (mostly religious) were invited by the five provincials to take part in this program, which began at La Salle College and then moved to the University of Notre Dame for its final three years. Participants received the degree of Master of Educational Administration from the University of Notre Dame.

Kit taught two courses, *Leadership in a Time of Crisis and Change*, and *Supervised Practicum for School Administrators*. The participants took prescribed education courses, such as curriculum development, school finances, teacher supervision, but overwhelmingly what they appreciated the most and remembered years later was the emphasis on the *Goals and Criteria* and the community that they built together.

Maria Buonato[50] was one of the students in the summer institute. She remembers both the program and Kit's role:

> Kit was a prophet, a prophet without honor. She had vision and was fearless in pursuing this vision. There were several key elements to the program: It was concrete and very practical, and bonds were formed among Sacred Heart educators from across the United States. We were Sacred Heart educators, not living in isolation; we could lean on one another. As the chief instructor of this program, Kit's depth of humor was evident as well as the depth of her spirituality. She invited renowned speakers to talk to the group, including Henri Nouwen.

In *Times Change*, her book about the Network of Sacred Heart Schools, Susan Maxwell[51] lists the following as *Society Seminar* topics and presentations: *Justice and the Church* by Joe Holland from the Center of Concern in Washington, D.C.; *The Society of the Sacred Heart through its*

[50] Maria Buonato, RSCJ, born in Philadelphia 12/10/1934, currently lives in Albany, New York, after having taught and administered in schools of the Society and other schools and worked in its retirement centers.

[51] Susan Maxwell, RSCJ, born in Evanston, Illinois, on 7/29/1941, followed Kit as the head of the Network. She served also as head of school at Bloomfield Hills, Michigan, and at Sheridan Road in Chicago.

General Chapters of 1964-1976 by Sisters Jean Ford, Catherine Lacey, Kit Collins, and Mavie Coakley; *The World and the Adolescent* by Dr. Marvin Schwartz; *How and Why Groups Change* by Sister Jean Bartunek; *Education and the Role of Women* by Sister Mary Quinlan; *The Development and Use of Resources for Mission* by Sister Nance O'Neil; and *The Search for Integrity Essential to Sacred Heart Education* by Father Roger Radloff. Kit sought the "best" to present the mission and charism of the Society to future Sacred Heart leaders. David Purpel,[52] a renowned educational theorist, was Kit's guru, whom she consulted for both content and context. He guided her and became not only a consultant, but also a friend.

On July 6, 1979, Kit wrote to her friend Vicky Uy,[53] the headmistress of the International School of the Sacred Heart in Tokyo, her impressions of the Summer Institute:

> The Summer Program at Notre Dame is going very, very well.... It is a real advantage to have international representation in the group, especially this summer when the focus of the *Summer Seminar*...is on the statement from the Assembly of Provincials in Mexico City in January 1979—*Education to Justice in Faith*. So far, we have had Mary Quinlan and Jean Ford, both of whom you know well, and Will Tabb, who did an analysis of capitalism and the implications of that for us as Christian educators. So it has been, as a whole, very, very thought provoking.

Margaret (Meg) Causey,[54] one of the Notre Dame participants noted, "Kit's bedroom was our community room." Meg cited Kit's chief characteristics as her ability to "bring people in"—into the group, into the process, into the discussion. "Kit was so creative; she was a woman of incredible vision, generous with her time and energy.... Kit so believed in herself, believed she was 'right' and in fact had to be right. She needed strong people around her to challenge her, to temper her opinions, to mellow her. For example, when someone did not

[52] David Purpel, scholar, educator, author of many books on education, especially from the point of view of ethics, was a consultant and friend of Kit and of the Society of the Sacred Heart whose schools he admired.

[53] Vicky Uy, former RSCJ, born in the Philippines on 8/9/1945, was principal of the International School in Tokyo in the 1980s.

[54] Margaret "Meg" Causey, RSCJ, born in Shreveport, Louisiana, on 6/2/1947, has served as teacher and administrator in Network schools, on the USC provincial team, and is currently on the Network staff.

go along with her, she would push; she did not give up." Meg noted, "Under the veneer of strength and humor, Kit protected her sensitivity. She was not one to show her vulnerability. She was a flamboyant person who played her cards close."

From 1976 to 1979, seventy-seven individuals, religious and a few lay colleagues, participated in and benefitted from this leadership institute. Kathleen Conan credits the Notre Dame program as one of Kit's major achievements and contributions to the Society and the Network. She recalled that in addition to the *Society Seminar,* Kit created community in the program, and of course, introduced periodic celebrations. To quote Meg Canty, "We worked hard, played hard, and prayed hard!"

Looking back, Kathleen Conan believes that Kit fostered the idea of uniting the five provinces through the schools. "If the schools were connected, personnel could exchange. The provincials believed it would be easier to start [unification] with an established entity, the schools."

Development of the Network

Kit knew that ownership of the members was necessary for the success of the Network. Annual meetings of heads and chairs of boards of trustees and of trustees were held. Kit also formed two standing committees to assist her and to ensure participation by the membership. The School Committee, composed of two heads, two middle managers, and two faculty members from across the Network, served as advisors to the Network director and helped develop programs for teachers and staff. As the Network evolved and times changed, Kit realized the need for a second committee to work with the technology directors and staff in each school. The Technology Committee was composed of individuals with the necessary expertise in technology from across the Network. Her goal was to make and keep Sacred Heart schools on the cutting-edge in this ever-changing field. Terri Goodwin[55] and Mary Jane Ferrier, and Kit herself were early members. Terri describes Kit, "as an astonishing educator, on the cutting-edge.... I truly believe Kit can be credited with the survival of the Sacred Heart schools in this country.... Kit was inspirational." She inspired confidence, and Sacred Heart educators across the country respected and followed her advice and guidance.

As the services of the Network increased, Kit needed a place to work. The Interprovincial School Office became successively the Network office and that of the School Committee. It was housed at first in the gardener's potting shed behind Newton Country Day School in Newton, Massachusetts. Although small, it served as the headquarters for the work that Kit was trying to accomplish. The

[55] Terri Goodwin, former RSCJ, born in Sandport, Idaho, on 12/12/1942, served as an educational consultant on technology.

apartment provided space for Kit and her secretary, Claire Shea, as well as a small meeting room and equally small space that could be used to produce publications and mailings. The Network Office remained at this location until it moved to 860 Beacon Street in Newton Centre.

Kit at her desk

Meetings of Heads of Schools

The first meeting of the heads of school occurred in March 1973 in Washington, D.C. At this meeting, the school heads defined the schools as a network "committed to education for liberation, justice, peace and faith," and pledged to be accountable to one another as they moved forward.

The *Goals and Criteria* were first approved in April 1975. In the 1975-76 academic year, all of the Sacred Heart schools within the United States were evaluated, but the process varied across the five provinces. A second meeting of heads of schools was held in August 1976 at Woodlands Academy in Lake Forest, Illinois, at which a structure and process for national accountability was recommended and approved. In February 1978, the five provincials approved the structure of the Network Commission on Goals (NCOG), which would later become the Sacred Heart Commission on Goals (SHCOG), and appointed seven members to serve on the commission, including one layperson. Thus began the evaluative process and cycles of self-studies, visits, and action plans in which the schools in the United States and Canada participate every five years.

The *Goals and Criteria* were revised in 1990 and again, in 2005. The latest revision involving changes to the criteria took place in 2020; a new version is planned every fifteen years thereafter. While the criteria were adapted to meet the changing needs of the world, the wording of the goals remained consistent. The 1990 edition expanded the application of the goals from Sacred Heart students primarily to all the constituents of the schools, students, faculty, administrators and staff, trustees, parents, and alumnae/i.

By 1982, when the five United States provinces merged, most of the schools had formed independent boards of trustees. Shortly thereafter, the first national conference for trustees was held in 1982

in Washington, D.C. In 1991, a board of directors was established for the Network of Sacred Heart Schools, consisting of heads, trustees, the provincial, and the Network director, *ex-officio*.

The purpose of the Network was to keep the spirit and tradition of Sacred Heart education alive, authentic, and open to new development. Kit knew that for tradition to be authentic, it must remain in contact with its original sources. The *Goals and Criteria* are a contemporary expression of the work of Saint Madeleine Sophie Barat, and its evolution through the centuries. The introduction to the 1990 update of the *Goals and Criteria* describes the goals as "ageless"—"the five elements" that have been the framework of Sacred Heart education since its beginning in 1800. They "express the values, the intentions, and the hopes of the Sacred Heart tradition, sharpened to meet the needs of a rapidly changing world." The *Goals and Criteria* are an articulation of the indispensable and essential elements of Sacred Heart education.

So what constitutes the indispensable and essential elements of Sacred Heart education? During the process of writing the *Goals and Criteria*, Kit had asked the retirement community at Oakwood in Atherton, California, to answer this question. These women had served in Sacred Heart schools for a collective 1,067 years, according to her calculations. After lively and thoughtful discussion, without any reference to the proposed *Goals and Criteria*, they identified five interrelated qualities that, taken together, they believed constituted the tradition of Sacred Heart education: faith, social awareness, a critical consciousness, and active and responsible citizenship of an interdependent world. Kit commented:

> Each time I read through the *Goals and Criteria*, I begin to see more clearly that they root the Network of Sacred Heart Schools in a fifth quality that the community [at Oakwood] identified—some used terms, such as balanced, holistic, integrated—I'm going to call it the mystery of paradox, the struggle, the tension of being both/and, of finding an identity and integrity in the heart of seemingly contradictory truths.[56]

In his book, *The Prophetic Imagination*, Walter Brueggemann[57]

[56] Unpublished talk to the Oakwood community.
[57] Walter Brueggemann is a noted American Protestant Old Testament scholar and theologian.

describes the role of the prophet as "to nurture, nourish, and evoke a consciousness and perception alternative to the consciousness and perception of the dominant culture around us." The prophet looks at the world that is and proclaims, "There is another way." Kit was a prophet who found another way, and led the schools in a new collaborative direction. With undaunted courage, Kit forged a new future for the schools of the Sacred Heart.

The Network is growing and thriving today because of the genius of Kit Collins. Uniting Sacred Heart schools across the United States under the *Goals and Criteria*, Kit created infrastructures to sustain the unity, such as the accountability process (SHCOG), the heads' biannual meetings, the trustees' conferences, and ad hoc committees that bring faculty and staff together around common interests and issues. It is indeed a living testimony to her genius that the Network is flourishing nearly fifty years later and has been emulated in Europe and Asia.

When Kit began the Network, she saw the possibilities of the dream articulated in the 1975 Preamble to the *Goals and Criteria*: "Independent but never isolated, every Sacred Heart school needs to feel the strength of belonging to a larger whole, of sharing principles and values, broad purposes, hopes, and ambitions." What began as a possibility was now well established as the Network of Sacred Heart Schools. Kit had given her life-blood to its founding, but the time had come for others to move it into the next century. Her prophetic role of was accomplished.

Contribution to the International Society

In 1976, Kit was elected as a delegate from the Washington Province to the Society's General Chapter in Rome. All delegates were urged to visit another province of the Society before their arrival in Rome, in order to expand their worldview, experience something of the international Society, and become acquainted with other members of the Society. Kit chose to go to the Province of Uganda/Kenya; this experience in Africa marked her heart and her soul forever afterward. Going to the chapter with a visit to Africa might seem like an interruption to her work as Network coordinator, but in reality, it changed her worldview and enhanced her perspectives and attitudes. The short visit to Africa stole her heart, colored her vision, challenged her thinking and her actions, and rooted her squarely in the struggle for peace and justice. The community on Otis Street in Washington where she lived for so many years still has artifacts she collected on that trip. Perhaps it was the stark difference of lifestyle, perhaps a call within herself to emulate the simplicity that had touched her life, or maybe it was the crying need for education in Uganda that inspired and shaped her thinking and attitudes.

When she returned from the Chapter, she visited the Network schools in the U.S., showing slides of Uganda. In sharing her Ugandan and Kenyan experience with the Network, Kit enlarged the world for her colleagues. The author of this biography, a long-time RSCJ Network member, remembered:

> The first time I met Kit was when she visited the school I was working in, and she talked to the children about Uganda. The slides she showed were fascinating. I never imagined children going to school in such circumstances. Eight years later, after my profession, I visited Uganda and

CATHERINE COLLINS, RSCJ (1937 – 2010)

taught English in Kenya for two months. I am sure it was seeing Kit's slides and hearing her presentation that spurred me to go to Africa! She had expanded my world and enabled me to embrace differences.

Lolín Menéndez remembers Kit's visit to Africa before the 1976 Chapter:

My first "real" contact with the "real" Kit took place in the early 1970s. I was teaching in the lower school at Carrollton. Kit came for the faculty workshop before the start of the school year. She had us, lay faculty and nuns, working together, engaged in a process of reflection that I did not know was the seed of the *Goals and Criteria*. Kit foresaw the decline in numbers of RSCJ in the schools and began to involve all of us in a sharing of who we were and why, a sharing of our roots and spirituality, the passing on of the charism.

Kit was elected delegate of the Washington Province to the General Chapter of 1976. She chose to have an experience of life in the Society in Africa, an experience that turned into an adventure and marked her for life. Kit visited the remote region of Karamoja in Uganda where the RSCJ had made a reality the desire of the Chapter of 1970, "to go where others cannot or will not go." One afternoon, Kit and Ronnie Dewey accompanied Paulina López Ridruejo[58] on her visit to some outlying villages. But night fell quickly… and they were lost in a desert with no paths or landmarks. Kit relished showing a picture of what it was like, a slide of nothing but black. When in the following year I was sent to Karamoja, Kit's parting advice was, "Never, but I say NEVER, go anywhere with Paulina López Ridruejo. I heard Kit's voice each time I went to the villages with Paulina, especially the times when we did get lost!

Kit also visited the RSCJ in what was then Zaïre [the Democratic Republic of the Congo]. She was very ill during the chapter, and it was said that she had contracted the "green monkey disease" during that visit. The African connection remained very alive to the end of her days.

[58] Paulina Ridruejo, RSCJ, born in Zaragoza, Spain, on January 18, 1939. She was professed February 3, 1969, and serves in the Uganda/Kenya Province.

International Visits

As Network director, Kit was invited to visit Sacred Heart schools in various countries as a consultant. Her itineraries were packed; she always sought to give all that she could in the time she had. She attempted to consolidate trips and to save money. Kit organized her trips by date and place, group and purpose. The group included individual communities, specific persons, provincial teams, faculties and students. The "asked to" list, as Kit referred to it, was impressive in scope and range. During her ten years as the coordinator of the Network of Sacred Heart Schools, Kit visited eighteen countries. She travelled at the invitation of the schools to talk about a myriad of topics: the Network in the United States; the uniqueness and value of Sacred Heart education; best practices in education and organizational models; justice and faith in Sacred Heart schools, and the internationality of Sacred Heart education. In high demand, occasionally she had to decline a request, but her schedules attest to her non-stop travels around the world. Just reading her itineraries at times is exhausting! Her energy, her generosity, and her passion for education filled her talks.

From 1976 to 1980, her visits included Ireland, Scotland, Austria, Germany, Japan, Zaire, Uganda, and Egypt. In 1980, Kit gave a leadership workshop at Craiglockhart College, Scotland, for educational administrative teams from Ireland, Northern Ireland, and Scotland. She performed a variety of services for the provinces and schools she visited. Over time, the following tasks appear in her itinerary:

- Gave an educational presentation in the Philippines
- Facilitated a process and design for the Malta district assembly
- Worked with both the Sacred Heart schools and religious communities in Japan, as well as the Sacred Heart University in Tokyo

- Worked with the schools, the faculty, administration, alumnae, trustees, and religious communities in Korea
- Gave faculty workshops on Sacred Heart "Education and Values" in Ireland, Scotland, and Northern Ireland
- Gave workshops for principals, trustees, and the Education Committee in Australia; worked in the Sacred Heart schools in New Zealand with faculty, administration, alumnae, trustees, as well as the religious communities
- Was on the keynote panel of AMASC (Worldwide Association of Sacred Heart Alumnae) in San Francisco.

On her trip to the Far East in the spring of 1980, Kit traveled to Korea, Japan and Taiwan. Visits to Australia and New Zealand followed. Prior to each visit, Kit mailed packets of material tailored to the particular country and school, its needs and desires, so that participants would be prepared for her visit and therefore more able to benefit from her time with them. In April 1980, Kit sent a comprehensive list of topics she could talk on to the International School in Tokyo. The topics ranged from the Myers-Briggs self-inventory to workshops on *Education to Justice* and *Goals and Criteria Assumptions*. Before Kit's arrival in Japan, Ruth Sheehy,[59] the headmistress, described a typical day at the International School, which was meant to give Kit a picture of life in the school. It could have frightened a less-experienced administrator. Sister Sheehy wrote:

> We are now into the last lap of the school year, having recommenced after Easter with a "typical" day at International School of the Sacred Heart.

1) Before the morning teachers' meeting at 8:10 a.m., one teacher drew me aside in tears to say that a very dearly loved aunt had died suddenly in the U.S., and would I ask for prayers. She was in her early 60s. Her tears were no sooner dried than another teacher opening her Easter mail in the faculty room found out that her aunt, aged 52, had died in England!

[59] Ruth Sheehy, RSCJ, born in Ireland on 5/8/1926, was headmistress of the International School in Tokyo from 1980 to 1996.

2) Towards mid-morning, we had a phone call from the police to say that one of our children was likely to be a kidnap case and would we be extra careful.

3) At noon, the health authorities phoned to say that one of our families, who had been vacationing in the Philippines, had developed dysentery and that they were sending out a squad to disinfect the school. And to watch out for a few days.

4) At dismissal time, two kindergarten children were missing, and we had just phoned the police when they were discovered hiding in the teachers' toilet.

5) In the course of the afternoon, I had a call from a "Kramer vs. Kramer" family requesting me to find evidence in their case!

Sister Sheehy concluded with one telling sentence: "By the end of the day, I was fully aware that school was in session again!"[60]

Kit visited the International School of the Sacred Heart in Tokyo several times as the coordinator of Sacred Heart Schools in the United States. She admired and respected the headmistress, Ruth Sheehy, and thought the education given there was innovative and challenging. After another trip to the International School, Kit wrote:

First of all, I have to say that I found myself tremendously challenged and enthusiastic about both the meaning and possibilities of the International School, because I believe that the contemporary world is in need of a very deep-reaching kind of interdependence. More than that, interdependence based on faith is perhaps the only hope for the future of a world so painfully and destructively divided and one in which autonomy has taken its toll. Further, I think such a school takes on special significance in the light of the insight, the direction, and the commitment of the 1976 General Chapter with regard to internationality, the building of communion, and a deep sense of the link between education and justice. I believe that the Chapter of 1976 provides a wonderful, rich, and profound (a) confirmation of the place for such an apostolate as the International School in the Society, and (b) challenge for organic growth and change for the school to become

[60] Ruth Sheehy to Kit Collins, 4/19/80.

increasingly international in its structures, its program and, of course, its spirit.

At the conclusion of this long, six-page letter, giving her reflection, Kit again lavished praise on the International School:

> After all is said and done, let me say once again, that I treasure my days at the International School, as some of the richest, most interesting, and challenging of my experience. I loved the Community whose warmth and welcome really touched me. I enjoyed to no end talking with and being with the faculty and students, and felt very much at home among them. I was enormously struck by the tremendous possibilities I found there, especially in light of the Chapter of 1976. I have only admiration for what you and P.C.[61] have accomplished in the past several years with the help of some dedicated religious and lay colleagues. I felt very much with you in the difficulty of living with the uncertainties of staffing an International School for the Society and living with all the surprises that that kind of school inevitably brings. Yet those are the things that make up the reality of its challenge. Sincere thanks for giving me the opportunity to be part of it for those days.[62]

A summary of her visit to New Zealand concretized the impact she had on the groups she worked with. During the course of her days in New Zealand, Kit spoke to faculty and staff, alumnae, students, and parents. She entitled her talk, "The Faces of Sacred Heart around the World," and, according to the recorder of the account of the workshop, "it was this face of the internationality of the Sacred Heart for alumnae, students, parents, staff, and religious that deepened for them their understanding of Sacred Heart education, its uniqueness, its legacy, its gifts." Kit shared her understanding and passion for mission with faculty and staff, parents and students, whether giving a formal talk or meeting informally with various groups:

> Not long ago someone said to me, "Well, you are a teaching order, aren't you?" And I replied, "As a matter of fact, no.

[61] Patricia Culhane, RSCJ, an Irish religious, born 3/17/1909, was assistant head of the International School in Tokyo.
[62] Letter to Ruth Sheehy, 1/4/77.

I wouldn't say that we are a teaching order, but we are an educational order." Difference in time and place will mean that the shape of our commitment, the way that education takes place, will differ enormously. The education of people from a religious and spiritual point of view—intellectual, moral, aesthetic and physical—will vary. Being true to our commitment to educate in faith is going to demand something very different in Poland, Rome, Taiwan, Korea, Uganda, or Wellington, but for 180 years our commitment has been to educate the whole child, the whole person, and that remains.[63]

These words conveyed the understanding of and deep commitment of the RSCJ to their mission of education. Kit instructed her audience on the universal mission of education with wide knowledge, warmth, common sense, deep spirituality, and infectious humor.

One of her greatest gifts was to bring new vitality and meaning to the internationality of the Sacred Heart. Kit had the ability to convey a sense of the many and varied ways in which the RSCJ were carrying out their mission and sharing their commitment as educators in many locations. Kit talked from her own experiences, often illustrating her talk with slides taken on her travels bringing people and places alive for her audience.

The changes in the Society, precipitated by the decrees of Vatican II, were still causing concern in the 1980s, especially for some alumnae of Sacred Heart. Often the religious were seen as "deserting" the schools and abandoning the people associated with the institutions. In formal talks or at her individual visits with the different constituencies of a school, as well as in informal encounters, Kit educated them to an understanding of the call of the church to the Society after Vatican II. One alumna admitted, "I could never understand why the nuns seemed to be giving up the schools, but now I began to see that they were moving into other kinds of education, and not abandoning them at all." Kit was, in fact, teaching the decrees of the Second Vatican Council, as its decrees directly influenced the mission of the Society, and, therefore, the ministry of the schools. She was able to explain how these decrees influenced the schools. She was able to listen attentively to concerns and frustrations and to provide explanations and reasons for changes

[63] Talk to Educational Advisory Committee, New Zealand, 5/21-22/80

in the Society. Thus, Kit became an ambassador of the Society of the Sacred Heart as well as the Network of Sacred Heart Schools. She carried the message of Sacred Heart education and the Society to each place she visited. Sometimes her journeys were long, especially when she combined visits to several countries, such as Korea, Japan, and New Zealand in 1983. At other times, they were short, like her trip to Ireland and Scotland in 1980, when she and Susan Maxwell, RSCJ, travelled together for ten days or when she visited Malta for a week. But the format was always the same: materials would be sent in advance; Kit would give formal talks to specified groups; she then would work informally with other groups; and always, at the end, there was follow up. This period of Kit's life reads like a travelogue: Nairobi, Cairo, Rome, Paris, Seoul, Tokyo, Vienna, Frankfurt, Cologne, as well as other cities in Japan, the Philippines, Ireland, Australia, New Zealand, Taiwan, Malta, and Scotland.

Susan Maxwell and Kit

Kit's purpose on these trips was to assist the schools in living the mission of education in new and deeper ways, with each trip tailored to the needs of the particular school she was visiting. For example in Aberdeen, Scotland, in 1981, the key topics of her visit were successful administrative teamwork, effective communication, and making the best use of a teacher's gifts for the good of the whole. In 1987, Dr. Phil Dineen, the headmistress of the Woldingham School in England, asked her to lead a staff conference on the *Goals and Criteria* with

the goal to give a better understanding of the goals of Sacred Heart education and the acknowledgement of the role of Woldingham within the international network of schools. Again, Kit achieved her task through a keynote talk, small group discussions on the goals and their practical expression at Woldingham.

When visiting countries, Kit led workshops on understanding justice and education and even helped with the revision of the District Government Plan, which was formed to implement the criteria from the Mexico Assembly of Provincials in January 1979, the focus of which was *Education for Justice in Faith*. In Taipei, Kit was asked to give a workshop about the context in which Sacred Heart education is offered. She posed to the participants several questions about the world and education:

- What is education?
- What concerns me most about the world/society in which I live?
- What is the world I hope will come to be?
- If such a world is ever to come into being, it will depend on men and women who are committed to our mission.

The group in Taipei envisioned an ideal world described in the *Goals and Criteria*, a world in which people pay attention to human groups and needs, value life and creativity, learn from each other, and forgive each other, and share wealth and national resources. At the end of that trip to Taipei, Kit received a charming note from a student thanking her and asking her to send stamps to add to her collection!

Kit was the face of the Network internationally and in the United States. She communicated the mission of Sacred Heart education through talks, conversations, and personal visits. She was in high demand! In the aftermath of the changes in the Society of the Sacred Heart and therefore in the Sacred Heart schools. Kit was a beacon and guide in how to organize and operate an excellent school of the Sacred Heart. Her expertise was admired, and the articulation of her vision was clear and strong.

Combined with the actual visits was the correspondence before and after the visit—and all of this was before the email revolution! Kit often had correspondence with the head of school or a particular person in the school who had sought her advice.

In a letter written on January 3, 1983, to Mrs. Mercy Nolan, deputy

principal of Sacré-Cœur in Melbourne, Australia, Kit explained that she sent materials ahead of her actual visit to ensure that she could meet the needs of the school:

> As far as my time is concerned, I am quite used to a full schedule and that would be fine. It is important that into that full schedule gets built solid time for my own reflection and planning. Preparation is most important to me. So please don't be hesitant about schedule provided that, within it, I will have time to do immediate preparation for whatever you would like me to do.

This summarized Kit's rationale for visiting schools: to be of service to the school in whatever way was most helpful to the personnel.

In summary, it can be said that for ten years of her life, Kit focused her creativity and energy on creating and developing the Network of Sacred Heart Schools in the United States, and in sharing this work with the schools in other countries. With the help of colleagues, lay and religious, she conceived the Network and launched it confidently on a steady course into the future. In October 1998, Catherine (Kay) Baxter,[64] former headmistress of Newton Country Day School in Newton, Massachusetts, gave the keynote address at the National Trustees Conference in Atherton, California. In her speech, she praised Kit's foresight in creating the Network:

> The Network is growing and thriving today because of the genius of Kit Collins. Uniting Sacred Heart schools across the United States under the *Goals and Criteria*, Kit created infrastructures to sustain the unity, such as the accountability process (SHCOG), the heads' biannual meetings, the trustees' conference, and ad hoc committees that bring faculty and staff together around common interests and issues. It is indeed a living testimony to her genius that the Network flourishes some twenty years later, and has been emulated in Europe and Asia.

[64] Catherine Baxter, RSCJ, born in Providence, Rhode Island, on 11/16/1928, was headmistress of Newton Country Day School from 1978 to 1989, then administrator of Oakwood from 1997 to 2004, where she died in 2009.

International Society Involvement

In addition to her work with schools within the international Society, Kit also participated in or facilitated several international meetings, such as general chapters, a provincial assembly in Malta and an international commission on education.

In 1976, Kit was elected from the Washington Province to attend the General Chapter in Rome. The General Chapter was the highest governing body of the Society, composed of delegates from each province. The General Chapter met every six years, and was responsible to set the direction and priorities for the international Society and to elect the next superior general, who would lead the Society during the next six years.

Helen McLaughlin, later superior general, gave us this picture of Kit at the chapter:

> Kit was a delegate at the 1976 Chapter and played an important part in it. When she arrived, she was unwell, due in part, I think, to all the traveling she did in Uganda over rough roads, etc. If I remember correctly, she was in the group who worked on government at the service of mission. She was the one who gave the simple diagram— recommendation leading to decision then on to action and assuring evaluation after a time. This is simple, but I know several provinces that used it. I was Provincial of Uganda/ Kenya and we used it there.

The diagram credited to Kit by Helen outlined her beliefs about responsibility, obedience, authority, discernment, and government. For her, government was rooted in discernment and built on participation. The key for her was participation and process by those whom the decision affects.

The 1976 Chapter mirrored the society. "These are difficult times,

and times of great hope as well. Let us keep on trusting in her (Mary's) presence which confirms us: in faith, in generous love, in the joy of the gift freely given." (1976 Chapter). Sisters no longer lived in a cloistered setting as it had been lifted in 1967, and the Society was struggling to discover how to live religious life without the trappings (the habit, cloister, an order of day (daily schedule) associated with it). The 1976 Chapter called for a commitment to live contemplation "in truth," to build communion within the Society and with others, to work for justice with the heart of an educator in a world torn apart by suffering, and to discern God's will. All of these summonses were part of Kit's nature. These virtues were innate in her very being; they were part of her essence, so, of course, they resonated in her.

Kit diligently working at the 1976 Chapter

In the early 1980s, Kit facilitated the District Assembly of Malta. Malta was a province whose population was composed of RSCJ who administered and taught in the school and coadjutrix sisters who performed the domestic duties. The latter were an elderly population, most of whom had not gone beyond a high school education.

In 1985, Kit facilitated the new provincials' meeting, called by the general council to bring the newly appointed provincials together for training, information sharing, and community building among themselves.

In 1994, although Kit was not a delegate at the General Chapter, held near Ottawa, she made an important contribution. She was asked to offer the services of the CEDC to document the Chapter on video.

She went there with an assistant from the Center and filmed, not only the official events but also various celebrations; she also conducted interviews about the chapter process with the participants and staff. Disappointed that she was not an elected delegate, according to Georgie Blaeser, a team member at the time, Kit nevertheless rendered a valuable service.

International Education Commission

Helen McLaughlin, superior general of the Society from 1982 to 1994, and her council formed the International Education Commission (IEC) to review the state of the Society's educational mission and named Kit as chair. Helen and Kit had first met in Rome during their probation. Helen became an admirer of Kit, whom she remembered not only as a hard-working and creative person, but also as one who liked to have fun:

> When, at the General Council, we saw there was a need to set up a commission to study, reflect upon our education, mainly formal education, at international level, it was very clear to me that Kit was the one to head this commission. She accepted and the international commission, with each continent represented, was formed. In part, thanks to Kit's ability, they worked together happily and produced a great booklet. I do not remember the title as we always referred to it as "The Gray Book," since the cover was gray.[65]

> The "Gray Book" is the International Education Commission's working paper entitled: *Education: A Commitment (IEC* document*)*.

> Whenever a meeting of this Commission was scheduled for Rome, we invited Kit to arrive early so that we, the General Council could have time with her; it took the form of facilitation that she offered. Even though her workload in the states was heavy, she always accepted to come and was a breath of fresh air, always in great form, upbeat and bringing new ideas.

[65] Letter of Helen McLaughlin to the author of this biography.

The commission was composed of an international group of RSCJ educators: Kit Collins (USA), Judy Garson (USA), Marie Noronha (India), Isabel Rodriguez (Northern Spain), Shona Garcia (Chile), Ada Martinez (Cuba), and Marie Guyonne du Penhoat (France). In the letter to the communities that accompanied the final document, the commission explained why and how it had used the input from the membership of the international Society:

> It became clear to us through the process that this is a special time for the Society; that as a Society we have begun to be changed, not by words of commitment promised, but by the lived experiences of choices made. We have found renewed conviction and energy about our call as educators; we have sensed deep hope in the assurance that we as a Society are moving and changing in response to God's call in the struggles of our time, while remaining true to the essentials of our tradition. At the heart of all this, we found real clarity on several important issues that face us as a Society today, and which have serious implications for our choices concerning apostolic priorities, those with whom and among whom we serve, our style of living, and our manner of service. In seeking to grasp more deeply the demands of our call to be educators, the membership of the Society has addressed these points.
>
> In this Working Paper, we have tried, in spite of the limitations of time and language, to express what we have learned from you, with integrity and insight.

The document, according to the commission, was a collaborative effort of the whole Society, characteristic of Kit's inclusiveness. It begins with a picture of the Society of the Sacred Heart: "An Apostolic Community: A Reflection":

> From the Society's reflection over the last two years, we have attempted to express a collective image, a mosaic, if you will, of the Society as an apostolic community today. Its style is quite different from what follows in the other sections of this paper. It will provide the basis for a video presentation of the Society, which will be available to provinces sometime in the next few months.

What follows is a poetic picture of the face of the Society. The reflection eventually would form the basis for the video, "Seeking the Face of God," which Kit created through the Center for Educational Design and Communication. The first several verses portrayed a "dark picture of the world" on the threshold of the Third Millennium:

> In every corner of the world, we see the same images. They are world images, images of crisis, broken promises and broken people. Cultural domination, oppression of women, disintegrating social fabric, militarism. Images of despair across all age lines, unemployment, racism, economic exploitation, violence, images of drugs, broken families, meaninglessness, the rich get richer, the poor get poorer.

The tone changes with an affirmation of "images of hope," as RSCJ search for the face of God with patience and urgency, in the contradictions and the paradoxes of their vocation The introduction acknowledges the claim the world has on them, their love, their forgiveness, and their contemplation. The contradictions and paradoxes of being a Religious of the Sacred Heart are named:

> To be here and not able to be elsewhere
> To be here now and unable to remain here tomorrow
> To live among the poor and to have more than they,
> To live as we are called to live and not to have the means to
> do that to which we are called
> To criticize injustice, and be unable to overcome it,
> To have too much and be ashamed to be givers,
> To want to give strong pledges to stay
> and be humble enough to leave.
> To pour out our energies and to hold back enough to be
> given,
> To be penetrating in our education and
> restrained enough to be educators.
> To be resolute in our convictions, yet vulnerable to be
> changed
> by events, words, deeds not our own,
> To be sensitive to the wounds of our world, yet convinced
> enough not to be paralysed by the pain we see and feel,
> To shape institutions for the strength they can bring,
> but not to be held back by their weight

To be faithful to our Church and insist that it be different
To maintain our personal and cultural identity, and be one
 international community – Religious of the Sacred Heart.

Whether in formal education, in parishes, in ashrams, in hospitals, or in retreat centers, RSCJ are "Called to be...wanting to be true educators, women of faith, of communion, of learning."

Wherever we are we commit ourselves
as educators
to a broad critical vision of the world
enlightened by faith,
intellectual discipline,
directing our energies and our choices
to actions,
to a way to be,
a way to bring something new into being,
to nourish life.

Here in embryo are the goals of Sacred Heart education! Here is the heart and soul of what Kit believed: To be a Sacred Heart educator was to have a broad, critical view of the world, enlightened by faith and intellectual discipline that directs one's energies and choices to a new action that would nourish life.

The introduction concludes with a prayer asking to seek "the face of God in the wounds of humanity...and to know the love of God in the healing of those wounds."

We ask
what it asks of us—in God:
 to purify our vision,
 to tame our ways of violence, of selfishness, of competition,
 to nourish the seeds of risk, of courage, of faithfulness,
 and to share our goods, whatever we have;
 to tend to our gifts of service—of mind, of heart,
 of body, of spirit.

Convinced that Christ lives
in our sisters and brothers,
and in a special way
in the poor,

we are willing to risk
a new step forward
in salvation history,
side by side with others
embracing the Cross,
sure of the Resurrection.

Even today, educators in the international network of schools still refer to the insights of the International Education Commission. Kit's voice was heard in every line. Helen McLaughlin recalled the value of these documents: "Recently, when I was asked to give a retreat, I arrived a few days early, and what was my delight to see two younger sisters discussing the Gray Book. It contains much that can be of help to those teaching today." Helen remarked also that Kit did not create *Seeking the Face of God* on her own, but she did lead its production and influence its direction. Reflecting on the process of writing the IEC paper, Helen continued

> It seems to me that the IEC document is having a stronger impact now than it did when it was published in 1988.... In light of the Chapter mandate to articulate the Society's educational mission, many people, especially young RSCJ, have gone back to read and study the IEC, realizing that it captures our educational mission as lived with many faces and "on the ground" experience of the world. It was a visionary work that unsettled some when it was published, but continues to this day to stand as a true insight into (or reflection of) the Society's educational mission.

The document revealed a face of our educational mission that encompassed not just formal education but the many ways RSCJ and our colleagues live the mission. Like much of Kit's work, the IEC document has stood the test of time and changed the minds and hearts of many Sacred Heart educators, providing them with a wide worldview.

International Education Commission - 1986
L to R: Marie-Guyonne de Penhoat (FR),
Judy Garson (USA), Ada Martinez (VEN),
Kit Collins (USA), Marie Noronha (IND),
Shona Garcia (PER), Isabel RodriQuez (Zaire)

Kit with the members of the International Education Committee

Kit nourished and developed the Network from its inception. She created the concept of a network of Sacred Heart schools and led its growth, until in ten short years it became an educational force in the United States and was known around the world. Kit's contribution to education—and to the mission of Sacred Heart education—was immeasurable. But after ten years as national coordinator of Sacred Heart schools, Kit was asked to begin a new venture for the community.

Center for Educational Design and Communication

In August 1984, when Kit knew that she was transitioning to the Center for Educational Design and Communication, she wrote Josephine Borg in Malta:

> I will be moving in a few weeks to Washington, D.C., where I am to begin an Education and Communications Center for the Province. It will be a sort of further development of the various kinds of work that I have been doing for the Society and should be a very challenging new venture for all of us.

According to Nance O'Neil, RSCJ, then the provincial of the United States Province, Kit was "the only one" who could begin this new venture, the Center for Educational Design and Communication. Nance O'Neil remembered the day Kit agreed to begin the CEDC:

> I vividly remember the morning Kit said "Yes" to creating what turned out to be the CEDC. We'd had the rich young man for the reading at Morning Prayer. Kit didn't share in the provincial house chapel, but right after, she came to my office and said with tears, "I can't go away sad because of my many precious possessions. I'll see what I can do in communications."

Kit's acceptance of this new ministry was another example of her living the call of the *devise* given to her in probation, to accept willingly what was asked of her despite her attachment to the work she was currently doing in the Network of Sacred Heart Schools.

Rosemary Bearss,[66] a provincial team member at the time, insisted that Kit accepted the position out of obedience. Kit wanted to serve the Society wholeheartedly. With tears, she accepted this new ministry. When she did, she left behind her work in the Network completely. She put her hands, as it were, to a new plow and never turned back. For Kit, serving as director of the CEDC was primarily a matter of vocation:

> That I am here at the Center to begin with is a matter of vocation for me, the fruit of a very real discernment that called me to begin a new work here. More importantly though, vocation to me is a vital, all alive, colorful changing daily thing, in the struggle for faithfulness to the gentle inner voice, the compelling perspective of faith, the needs of our world, the relationships brought into being here as sign and sacrament. It is an insistent call, one I share with the whole Society, to communion.[67]

At this time, the community living at 821 Varnum Street in Washington, composed mainly of elderly RSCJ, was "withering," according to Rosemary. Nance thought the building could be used as the new home for the CEDC. The Society owned the building and was willing to renovate it to accommodate the needs of the CEDC. Betty Shearman[68] was charged with the repairs from heat to AC, plumbers to phones. She quickly became the "go-to" practical person, the "hands and feet" of this new work. In the beginning, she went to the army supply store to furnish the offices, and later worked directly with Kit. Warren Davis was hired as a graphic artist, and with Betty's help, he set up a graphics room. Being an artist and photographer herself, Betty often took pictures and videos of the people, meetings, and activities in the Center, as well as outside the daily work place. From the beginning, Nance O'Neil involved Kit in the planning process, so Kit felt ownership of it.

Joan Gannon[69] recalls Kit as a "risk-taker," who demonstrated this

[66] Rosemary Bearss, RSCJ, born in Portland, Oregon, on 10/29/1931, was a member of the provincial team, later provincial of the United States Province from 1988 to 1993.

[67] RSCJ Journal, Summer 1987.

[68] Betty Shearman, RSCJ, born in New York on 7/8/1927, educator and artist, died at Teresian House on 3/31/2018.

[69] Joan Gannon, RSCJ, born in Washington, D.C., on 1/21/1936, educator and later a member of the provincial team, now works with retired RSCJ.

quality by accepting this new assignment. Once again, Kit was asked to create an entity out of nothing. She brought all her intellectual prowess, creativity, imagination, and organizational skills to the development of the CEDC, and she took it beyond the expectations of the leadership of the United States Province of the Society.

The province established the Center in September 1984. From the beginning, its purpose was to serve faith-based groups working for social justice and to offer communications skills to organizations that might not otherwise afford such services. The work of the Center was expressed in its mission statement:

> The Center for Educational Design and Communication (CEDC) provides affordable communication services and conference facilities to community and social justice organizations. Committed to the work of education through the empowerment of people, the Center emphasizes a strong sense of partnership in mission, a sensitivity to the diversity of experience, a willingness to engage in issues at depth, a collaborative style, and an attentiveness to communication strategy in the change process.

The services of the CEDC encompassed a wide range of communications and design services, including everything from branding to website design and multimedia presentations to project planning. The CEDC was founded also to provide strong educational and communications support to the Society of the Sacred Heart, both nationally and internationally. There was nothing small about what Kit undertook for the Society!

The staff of the Center for Educational Design and Communication

In a report to the provincial team in 1999, Kit listed the following accomplishments. The CEDC:
- guided and produced three editions of *Connections: Toward a Global Consciousness*; the three editions dealt with the key issues of refugees and migrants, enculturation and its impact, and the relationship of faith and politics.
- worked with the International Education Commission, engaging the Society membership internationally in a process designed to reshape our educational mission; the effort resulted in the IEC Working paper on Education, Society of the Sacred Heart.
- worked with the Provinces of Australia/New Zealand and Canada in producing a video on the Chapter of 1994, held in Ottawa.
- worked with the Canadian provincial to design, develop and launch a web site for the Province of Canada.
- worked with the International Justice and Peace Commission in developing and publishing the Social Justice Resource Book provided to the whole Society earlier this year.
- worked with the International Commission on the Bicentennial on the publication of the Spiritual Journey, in many languages, which will be an important resource throughout the Society for our reflection, prayer and communion during the Bicentennial year.

- assisted in process design for engaging the province membership in the discernment of current priorities for the United States Province, and in publishing the fruit of that discernment in *An Act of Hope*.
- offered hospitality to many RSCJ groups and committees during their working sessions.
- worked with the Technology Committee of the Province to strengthen our Mission through communication and to educate ourselves and others to the critical importance and faith-enlightened use of technology in the service of education, communion and social justice.
- in collaboration with the Technology Committee, created the province's web site (www.rscj.org), and assisted in providing Internet access and email for all communities in the province. The web site communicates a sense of the International Society; it provides a forum for RSCJ to exchange reflections on important issues, give news, ask for prayer and participate in decision making; it also includes a subsite for the Bicentennial, hosts the communication aspects of Mission Outreach, Volunteers in an Act of Hope, and the Associates' Program; it is linked with related sites such as the Network of Sacred Heart Schools and the Alumnae/i (AASH). In collaboration with the Bicentennial Committee is developing a brochure on the Society of the Sacred Heart."

It was an impressive volume of work for twelve months. None of these were *small* tasks. Regardless, questions swirled around the purpose of the Center and exactly what Kit was doing. There was intense speculation about her move from the Network to the CEDC in Washington, D.C. Was this new office and position created for her to help her move on from the Network? Was it the Society's way to ensure that the Network was held in "trust" by all its members? Was it simply time for Kit to use her talents in new ways? Where there is no knowledge, speculation ran rampant. Try as she might to explain, defend, or justify the work of the Center to the province, misunderstanding remained.

According to Paula Toner,[70] a former provincial of the United States

[70] Paula Toner, RSCJ, born in Tallahassee, Florida, on 6/22/1943, worked in Network schools as teacher and administrator, and later was provincial.

Province, the mission of the CEDC was to assist the provincial team in "searching for the variety of ways to make RSCJ reflections on our own experience accessible to others." Paula knew that she was able to do this. Kit herself shared her reason for undertaking this work of the Society:

> My conviction is that our work as RSCJ, whatever the work is, has to bear the character of being faith-based, loving, educative, relational, and global, at least in perspective. In other words, the very nature of the Society as an international congregation situates us, de facto, in the international community. Our collective history and "pact" with the Church compels us to respond, both personally and systemically, as educators, as empowers, and as sisters, especially to the suffering, the poor, the oppressed of our world today. We are meant, I think, to reveal love as a Godly force for the bringing together of the human community in fullness and freedom in some small way, however modest. Saying all of this reveals another one of my convictions; that while a religious vocation is a profoundly personal matter, it cannot be a private one. I believe that at the heart of religious vocation there is a really important social dimension that binds us one to the other, inviting our personal gift in shaping the response and vitality of the Society, as a community, in today's world.[71]

Kit goes on to disclose candidly her struggles beginning this uncharted ministry:

> For me personally, this is incredibly challenging and bears directly on the development of this Center as one way of responding. It is no secret how exciting (and sometimes how nightmarish) the creation of the Center has been, especially without any existing models on which to base our beginnings. We began with only a handful of people, a building, a statement of purpose, lots of commitment, talent, energy, faith and opinion! The lack of similar centers as reference makes it more difficult to write about.

[71] This and the following quotations are from personal letters of Kit's or from her private papers.

Many RSCJ in the province continued to be baffled by the work of the Center. Kit explained the purpose of the CEDC:

> What we bring to it is our own faith, an approach that is strongly educative, and a range of services, which run the gamut from group process and learning design, to communication strategy and production, to video duplication and hospitality. We do graphic design, video, audio and slide production, and consultation, on a whole spectrum of social concerns. And in doing, we attend to communication as a means of empowerment, of mediating relationships. It is perhaps the way of working out, at one and the same time, a theology of education and communication, and of joining our efforts to those of the larger community in seeking first the Kingdom of God and justice. There are lots of challenges: use of limited resources, inventiveness, working beyond privatized language, supporting common efforts without replicating works, and very specifically, struggling toward a social imagination that can believe a new order into being

In the 2007 winter issue of the Society's *Heart* magazine, Kit again provided the *raison d'être* for the CEDC. She believed that she was living the charism through her work at the CEDC.

> The charism of the Society of the Sacred Heart is to make known the love of the Sacred Heart of Jesus. To me, that means that the love of God is at the heart of really loving and caring for the earth, for those who are poor and marginalized. It is wanting to do the charism in a way that cares for those who are hidden—the least visible—and the outcasts.[72]

The work of the CEDC was supported by an enthusiastic and talented team, It is no coincidence that the CEDC staffers as a group reflected the social consciousness of their leader. For Kit the work was exciting, challenging, and transformative for the team and the Society as a whole.

The Center for Educational Design and Communications worked with many non-profits. Fifteen years after its inception, in a draft

[72] *Heart*, Winter, 2007, p. 14

statement of her vision for a book on the Society's ministries entitled, *Towards Tomorrow*,[73] Kit elaborated on the mission of the Center:

> In a nutshell, we at CEDC are in the active ministry of putting communication at the service of social change, social justice—of doing what we do from a profoundly educative perspective, of being a place of action, of communion and of hospitality. We work in partnership with under-resourced social change groups, people of passion and commitment who share something of the same vision, who work with few resources, and who, for the most part, have chosen to forego many benefits themselves in order to act in solidarity with those who are oppressed and marginalized, to press for educational transformation as integral to systemic change, and to use media as an agent of liberation giving voice, visibility, and power to those who have been denied. We approach our project partnerships with the belief that "media" is not about products, but about the thoughtful creation of effective and caring relationships; we struggle to use the "tools" of design to mediate relationships. We try to reflect in all that we do, the deepest meaning of our oft-repeated phrase, "Social Justice: It Happens by Design."

One of the many non-profits, with which the Center worked, the Morino Institute, will serve to illustrate its work. Mario Morino[74] was a philanthropist who wanted to invest in a non-profit that ministered to underserved populations. One branch of the Morino Institute was the Youth Development Collaboration (YDC). This pilot project engaged youth from low-income areas of Washington, D.C. It provided direct assistance in developing internet supported network learning centers and out-of-school programs for children in local neighborhoods, ages six to thirteen, who mostly were assigned to the worst of the city's schools. The CEDC worked with the YDC team to develop an inquiry-based project-learning curriculum, as well as a staff development program. For four years, Kit worked as an educational consultant directly with Tracy Gray, assistant to Mario Morino. According to

[73] Frances Makower: *Towards Tomorrow*, London, Darton Longman Todd, 2000, pp. 227-228.

[74] Mario Morino, Washington businessman and philanthropist who focused on after-school programs for children.

Tracy, Kit was practical, made the project seem possible, and could always find resources to supplement the program:

> What I most appreciated about Kit was her inclusiveness, her ability to create community. She brought myriads of people together. No one was treated as just an employee. She knew each one personally. The Morino Institute and Kit combination worked so well because Mario Morino understood technology and its power and Kit understood people. Mario was often referred to as a "stop and listen" person, and Kit as a "bring it on" person.

Kit was responsible for the strategic plan, working with the four centers of the Institute to strengthen technology, expand and update programs to be on the cutting edge, and train the staff. Since Kit was a visionary, Morino counted on her to develop the educational component of the program. A profile prepared for the Morino Institute staff stated on the cover: "To wire the machines is a job; to connect the people is an art." Mario believed Kit did both. Kit, according to Tracy, was "the north star anchor," and "a safe harbor," of the project.

Tracy and Kit became "wonderful friends." Tracy acknowledged that Kit was inclusive: "Kit knew each of her employees in a personal way…she would stand in front of a moving car for each one! She connected people, and connected the U.S. Province via email!" One of Kit's weaknesses, however, was finances. Tracy Gray summed up this area of Kit's life: "Kit was 'innovative' with budgets."

Eight years after Kit's death, Tracy reflected on her life and legacy. Her insights are profound and incisive:

> Kit was blessed with a brilliant mind that enabled her to explore a problem or dilemma with razor-like focus. Big or small, Kit would listen and begin to identify possible solutions to address the issue at hand. When we were dealing with a challenge of how to improve after school programs for underserved communities and ensure that the centers had the technology needed when funds were limited, Kit sounded the clarion call to business leaders in the area to donate their computers to be refurbished and distributed to programs in the region. She dogged and managed to get hundreds of technology tools into the hands of programs, students and their parents. If she knew that you had the

skills to repair the computers or the needed parts to enhance these machines, Kit would "encourage" you to help. Because of Kit's dedication, thousands of programs and families gained access to technology at a time when the digital divide was a barrier for many low-income communities.

Tracy explained Kit's passion for justice:

...it was that she was unapologetic about the need for equal justice for all citizens and made her views known without hesitation. She walked the walk and was not daunted by power, ignorance, and greed. She fought for those who had no voice and would not compromise when injustice was in her path. She was, in a word, fearless.

Kit was both friend and mentor, Tracy said:

Kit and I worked together at the Morino Institute under the inspired leadership of Mario Morino. Kit was part of Mario's inner circle identifying ways to improve the quality of after school opportunities for children in low-income communities. Because of Kit's deep knowledge about the Washington, D.C., region, its key players and programs, she was an invaluable resource to the creation of the Youth Development Collaborative (YDC). Through this effort, selected programs were provided financial and technical support to integrate technology into their school offerings. Kit dedicated her attention to the development of innovative training of leadership and staff to understand better how to leverage the power of technology. She was my thought partner and inspiration through the implementation of this groundbreaking initiative.

Tracy also cited Kit's work establishing an online network for the province as one of her most significant contributions. She said Kit's ability to communicate and bring people together was instrumental in the success of the project.

At a time when email was becoming part of everyday communications, Kit dedicated her attention [to] ensuring that everyone within the province had an email address and was connected to the online community. It is another

example of Kit's determination to make this possible and to provide the needed support to those who were just becoming familiar with the emerging technology tools and their potential to enhance communications within the community.

Citing Kit's sense of humor, which created community and sustained optimism, Tracy gives an example of her humor:

> Kit had the most contagious laugh of anyone I ever knew. She could find the humor in most situations and knew how to bring sunshine into the most difficult of circumstances. She was spontaneous and never missed the opportunity for a laugh. It was her optimism that shone through her humor. One of my fond memories of Kit was that we would exchange the same gifts, year after year, wrapped in different recycled packaging No matter how silly the re-purposed gift, Kit would throw her head back and howl with laughter at the clever packaging to fool the other person. It is difficult to describe, but we did this year after year, and it never got old. And it was always funny.

In conclusion, Tracy named Kit as her mentor, the person she wanted to emulate. Her wisdom and willingness to share it was boundless. She was the best friend one could ever hope for, always there to listen or provide gentle direction. Her mind was always open to ideas and her capacity to give of herself was remarkable. "When she passed, I felt such a tremendous loss. But I carry Kit with me each day, talking to her on a daily basis and know how blessed I am to have had her in my life."

While Kit's work with the Morino Institute served as an example of her work at the Center, more importantly, it served as an example of her great capacity for collaboration and friendship. Some, however, questioned this collaborative dimension of Kit, while others noted the price she paid for being such a communicator.

Betty Shearman recalled working with Kit at the beginning of the CEDC. Betty felt that after Nance and her team left office, few understood Kit or what she had been charged to do. Betty further stated:

Kit was a prophet, "without honor in her own country." She was a woman of great vision. She created the Network of Sacred Heart Schools based on goals and criteria that were a collaborative effort. As an excellent facilitator, Kit got input from all the schools. She saw the possibility of technology connecting. She helped the schools form independent boards of trustees, believing that, as stated in the introduction to the 1975 *Goals and Criteria,* each Network school was "independent but never isolated."

Betty also reflected on Kit's idea of using technology to connect the members of the province:

Kit's idea was to connect people, and the advent of the computer and the Internet provided the perfect means to do just that! The Internet offered a means to connect the members of the Society, letting them communicate one to one, province to members, schools to schools, groups to groups. The Internet, as a tool, could also aid other organizations that did not have the money to travel; it was a means to serve both the Society of the Sacred Heart and other organizations.

Two of Kit's far-reaching achievements and gifts to the Society through her work at the Center were to ensure that each community in the province had a computer and that each RSCJ had a personal email address. According to Meg Causey, Kit was convinced that each community should have an Apple computer. The provincial team, however, decided to leave the choice of PC or MAC to the communities and individuals. Kit also was quick to secure the domain "@rscj.org" to create individual emails for the members of the province. Each RSCJ email address had the same format, which remains to this day: firstinitiallastname@rscj.org. Having individual email addresses greatly enhanced communication within the province. It allowed members to connect with one another easily, and facilitated the leadership's ability to communicate with the entire province and with committees of the province. This helped solidify what had been five provinces into the single United States Province.

Georgie Blaeser observed, "Kit was a creative genius, but she had to rely on others for the technical expertise." Kit's two innovations, a computer in each RSCJ community and each RSCJ having her own

email address, pushed the Society of the Sacred Heart into the Internet age. But Kit had to rely on those at the Center with the technological expertise to implement her ideas.

Mavie (Margaret Mary) Coakley was asked to be a support to Kit at the beginning of the CEDC. In an internal interview conducted by the Center in 1989, Mavie admitted, "I am not an expert in any of these things going on. But I am a good second person to whatever they are doing."

In the same interview, Melanie Guste,[75] a member of the staff, said, "The work is done corporately and in collaboration. I am connected to each person that comes to the Center. Every single person who comes through here knows we are with them and stand with them. I have learned how to listen here." Asked what the value of the Center was, Melanie replied:

> The Center provides services that others don't have the funds to gain access to because they are so costly. That is why so many come to us… [because they] had no voice, because they can't afford this…this place gives them options. They are refusing by their lives to accept that things have to be the way they are…. We are all about how we see things. It's how people see what they see, how they see the issues that other people bring in here. I think that is the biggest impact we have…. So it is to be involved with groups other than RSCJ and to be joined with what was already common effort [for justice] on at least the part of some groups and individuals….

Kit's influence on others was undeniable. In fact, Melanie Guste, who as a young religious worked with Kit, credited a significant part of her professional development to Kit's guidance.

> I worked with Kit for five years following my return to the States in 1987 from living in the Philippine Islands and Rome. Pleased to be recruited to join the staff, I never anticipated that I would have my new position at the Center as an "Education Consultant/Design Specialist." With

[75] Melanie Guste, RSCJ, born in New Orleans on 12/8/1952, was an educational consultant and design specialist while working at the Center. She is currently headmistress at The Rosary in New Orleans.

Kit as a dialogue partner and far less arrogance, I began a steep climb towards personal integration and professional development.

Kit's persistent bias toward reflection and process pressed me to continued refinement of my approaches to education and understandings of organizational change. Her unwillingness to be "the expert," and her insistence that I probe my experience for its value and truth re-oriented my more traditional view of pedagogy and more institutional/bureaucratic orientation to development. While her androgynous posture seemed laborious and excessive to me at first, in time I appreciated the dignity and respect it communicated.

As a consequence of collaboration with Kit, new possibilities emerged with clarity of purpose. My passions now more focused, I began to cross-function, juggle and enjoy what I was doing at deeper levels than ever before. I discovered new "intelligences" focusing with "artistic" intention on the design of good questions and recognizing inquiry as foundational to development whether it be international, rural, economic, or human! My commitment to "clearing" my mind to be present is also residual of Kit's influence, as well as practicing dialogue free of preconceived outcomes or anticipated results.

I believe that it wasn't by accident that my path intersected with Kit's when it did, and I know that it has been forever changed as a result.

Barbara Moreau[76] worked at the Center for eight years. Recruited by Kit, Barbara was the cook and hospitality coordinator. Barbara saw Kit as talented and creative, a charmer and, at the same time, a taskmaster. Kit was not easily accepting of advice, but at the same time, she was generous to a fault. "She would "give you the shirt off her back." She had an idea a minute! Barbara contends that Kit felt neglected by the Network. Having "conceived and birthed" this new reality, she suddenly had no part in it. As a person who needed to be affirmed, she sometimes felt that lack of recognition deeply, but seldom showed it.

The lack of understanding in the province of the purpose of the

[76] Barbara Moreau, RSCJ, born in New Orleans on 6/10/1938, was the hospitality coordinator at the Center for eight years. She died on 7/27/2019.

Center was frustrating and at moments hurtful to Kit. Try as she might to clarify its mission, the Center seemed to have a mystery about it. Some of the misunderstanding revolved around the question of money. Annual provincial reports to the province showed significant sums given to the work of the Center, but the province saw no information about how this money was used. Systematic financial accounting was not one of Kit's strengths. Provincial after provincial was frustrated by dealing with her over money, and each one tried to help her to be transparent and accountable about the finances of the CEDC.

In 2007, when Paula Gruner, RSCJ,[77] a member of the provincial finance office, asked for information about the Center's finances, Kit wrote a blistering response:

> This is an increasingly frustrating and unnecessarily time-consuming process for all of us. Please send me, by tomorrow, the following:

> 1) the detailed spread sheet including everything you have done with the information we have sent you from CEDC, identified by account numbers-according to your directive, since last August;

> 2) a detailed breakdown of all salary information you have done for us since September 2006. This should include all costs, deductions, etc. for each member of our staff (please send this only to me).thanks.

> 3) copies of the monthly reports from Paychex since September '06

> I think it would be helpful to have this on a regular basis... with the assurance that this follows what is done in the same way for each cost center in the province, as well as an indication that costs belonging to Society owned property (building repair, buildings and grounds, etc.) were indicated.

> I must admit the constantly changing requests seem unnecessary.

[77] Paula Gruner, RSCJ, born in Lancaster, Ohio, on 2/16/1950, was a member of the provincial finance office.

You can be sure that Will is tracking down any errors in the bookkeeping—and you should surely be aware that many RSCJ, with good reason, don't understand the reports and communications coming from your office, about the CEDC. I think that if you can send us the information I am requesting—and do so on a regular basis—that will help us review your requests and the reports and be able to respond to so many supportive RSCJ accurately.

More later. Happy Eastertide. Gratefully,
Kit"

In addition to the RSCJ who worked at the CEDC, the staff was composed of three lay people, Beth Ponticello (1995), Will Simpson (2001), and Laryn Bakker (2003). Beth Ponticello was hired in 1995 as the art/design director. She had had no previous contact with nuns, and so Kit was a surprise. Beth saw the Center as an important gift for non-profit organizations that could not afford design services: "We helped a lot of nonprofits as well as the RSCJ in Africa and South America." Beth does not remember turning anyone away. According to Beth, "Kit trusted her staff. 'You are responsible,' she would tell us. If it was a good idea, it was accepted." The office itself was a symbol of the chaos of the creative process—there was paper all over it! "Kit was...always looking for the next project." She brought unlikely people together; for example, before the International Women's Conference, she gathered women from around the world at the Center.

Will Simpson was hired as office manager. Will recalls being interviewed by Kit, not realizing at first that she was a nun! Will remained at the Center for more than ten years. According to Will, "Kit was mission-focused; that was at the heart of all she did." Will also recounted that Kit was always concerned about others and would "go to the ends of the earth" for others. "Kit sought truth, and to that end, she was 'open and honest.'" She preached doing things once. She did not take "no," for she always thought there was a way. "She listened to people, and therefore, could serve them."

In 2003, Kit hired Laryn Bakker as the media designer. Laryn described Kit as a "mother hen" who was interested in all aspects of his life:

Kit was warm-hearted, generous, a great storyteller who always engaged others in listening. She gave me lots of

latitude. She urged us to stay current; she wanted the latest and the newest; she was always enchanted by the "as seen on TV" products. When she would get a new computer though, she sometimes would keep working as she did on the old one!

Kit's personality was big, and at times, she was not an easy person to work with. She could be very stubborn! But her gifts were also huge. She taught me to look at the world through the "eyes of the Spirit," not just to look at it through "default" eyes. And she taught me to be open to change, not to be fearful of it.

Laryn remembered a conversation about what would happen if the Center "died." Kit said that "as long as we are faithful, the Spirit will continue…. Kit believed in reading the signs of the times. She was constantly looking forward! It is a testament to this spirit of faithfulness that Kit fostered that the CEDC continues to serve the international Society and many other congregations and non-profit organizations.

Leadership in the Province

Because of her many gifts, Kit was asked to serve the Society locally, nationally, and internationally. She enjoyed this work, and was excellent at it. When the IPB, the five provincials of the United States were considering restructuring, even merging, they appointed a task force to develop a plan. Kit represented the schools on the Design Task Force. Kit and Agnes Hoormann,[78] representing finances, and Mary Catherine McKay, representing formation, served as resource persons throughout the restructuring process. Formed in October 1979, the members of the Design Task Force were Bonnie Kearney, Sharon Karam, Constance Campbell, Lisa Fitzgerald, Sally Furay, Carol Purtle, and Frances Tobin, all RSCJ. This group was asked to create two or more possible structures to present to the IPB by May 1, 1980. Action steps for this task included a questionnaire sent to the entire membership in the United States, to get each person's opinion on a variety of issues that had a bearing on restructuring; area meetings were scheduled that gave the IPB a chance to hear the thinking of RSCJ in different parts of the country.

[78] Agnes Hoormann, RSCJ, was at the time the provincial treasurer of the St. Louis Province.

An Act of Hope

Six years later, after the five U.S. provinces had in fact merged into one province and after many objectives of the merger had been achieved, Provincial Rosemary Bearss called the province into a strategic planning process on the first Sunday of Advent 1989. Sister Bearss said that for this planning process to work, "good organization, planning and social analysis" were necessary. She believed that the province needed to adopt an on-going method of decision-making based on the best convergence of three essential factors: the mission of the Society, the province's resources, and the needs of our country.

Kit was a natural choice to chair a committee to set in motion the strategic planning process. The other members were Georgie Blaeser, Meg Causey, Judy Garson, and Marilyn Mc Morrow.[79] Kit led the committee in a collaborative effort to create a strategic plan for the United States Province. Their mandate was to surface province priorities for strategic planning. *An Act of Hope* was the result.

The introduction to *An Act of Hope* says: "We seek the generosity and strength to choose the way with joy and even a bit of excitement; a unique opportunity invites us. Another will not come soon." It continues: "the orientation of the life and service of the province will be to identify the struggle of the poor and to work against racism, sexism, and violence of every kind." The reaction of the province was mixed: some groups focused on attitudes, while others focused on specified actions.

Kit was troubled by the resistance because she thought the province would wholeheartedly embrace the priorities of the plan. Part of the problem was the process used to gather the data; many found it

[79] Marilyn McMorrow, RSCJ, born in Providence, Rhode Island, on 2/18/1947, a faculty member at Georgetown University, she served on the committee for *An Act of Hope.*

"grueling." Discussions around difficult topics seemed endless. Several alternative designs were presented in order to get feedback. *An Act of Hope* states: "The call to contemplation, education, internationality, and discernment mark our vocations and touch our lives at all times. Our priorities are time-bound expressions of what they ask of us today (1992)." The priorities were expressed as "joining the struggle of the poor for resources and conditions essential for human well-being, recognizing that education is central to this effort and our vocation" and "working against racism, sexism and violence of every kind."

Years after *An Act of Hope* was published, Bonnie Kearney, RSCJ,[80] reflected: "*An Act of Hope* capitalized on the experience of being human, not on institutions. These attitudes were meant to penetrate our educational institutions. They could change our prayer also, as we were called to bring life to prayer, not prayer to life."

Marilyn McMorrow cautioned: "With *An Act of Hope*, you are marching right straight into the jaws of controversy/hell/redemption, when it comes to our beloved Kit!" Kit believed passionately in the ideas and ideals put forth in the document; for her there was no gray area. The writing of the document, therefore, was painful and tense. The picture of tension was captured at breaks when some members went outside, while others stayed inside. The reactions of the committee varied around the reactions in the province to the strategic plan.

The work of these two committees, the Design Task Force and the Strategic Planning Committee marked gigantic moments in the history of the U.S. Province. Both changed the face of the province, and both processes bear Kit's mark. They attest to her creativity, her collaboration, and her service to the mission of the Society. She not only could create and develop a plan, but also use it to thrust the RSCJ into a future that was visionary and attainable.

The publication of *An Act of Hope* provoked division in the province, however. A meeting of heads of school in 1992 was extremely tense because of the implications for the schools of the emphasis in the document on the poor and marginalized. Helen McLaughlin, then superior general, was visiting the United States and attended a session of the meeting. Margaret (Peggy) Brown,[81] then director of Schools

[80] Bonnie Kearney, RSCJ, born in Evanston, Illinois, on 2/17/1943, had been a member of the *Design Task Force*.

[81] Margaret "Peggy" Brown, RSCJ, born in Lancaster, Pennsylvania, on 2/15/1927, was at the time director of Schools of the Sacred Heart in Atherton. She died at

of the Sacred Heart in Atherton, California, did not hesitate to put the question raised by *An Act of Hope* on the table: *Do the schools live the mission of the Society?* Sister Brown wanted to hear from the "top" (the superior general). She immediately responded "Of course!" but many school heads, of whom a number were RSCJ, still felt their efforts to administer the schools were unappreciated. It seemed that the strategic plan valued ministering among the poor over ministering in traditional Sacred Heart schools. Sister Brown had called the question, and the answer from Helen McLaughlin was an affirmation of the schools as an important expression of the Society's mission.

The social analysis process used to gather the data "moved the province forward," according to Rosemary Bearss. Kit designed the process and, according to Sister Bearss, it was "the right process," and Kit had been the right person to lead it. Diane Roche[82] believes *An Act of Hope* captured who Kit was. "She was a prophetic figure who called us beyond. *An Act of Hope* posed uncomfortable questions, and today still influences us as the gospel does." Even though it had a polarizing effect in the province, it gradually changed the way the Society worked for justice and called the members of the United States Province, wherever they were working, to "contemplation, education, internationality, and discernment."

Oakwood on 11/12/1995.

[82] Diane Roche, RSCJ, born in Boston on 12/31/1949, educator and social activist and member of the provincial team 2018 to 2021.

A Visionary

Many speak of Kit as a prophet. A year after Kit's death, Marie-Louise Wolfington[83] found among Kit's papers a reflection for Wednesday, February 18, 2015, entitled, "A Self-Balancing System." She marked it with the words, "This reminds me of Kit."

> In the Hebrew Scriptures, the central institution of Temple sacrifice, priests, and Levites attempted to balance itself with prophets, or the legitimation of official, sanctioned critics, even though they usually killed them in the end. But at least the immense prestige and authority of ritual and priest craft was balanced by the charismatic authority of the truth-speaking prophets. One was inherited and ascribed status, the other was earned by speaking truth with no formal legitimation ever possible (Deuteronomy 18:9-22). There is no ordination for a prophet. So you can perhaps sense the inherent tension between prophets and priests, and also between prophets and kings (2 Samuel 12:1-7). Kings and priests were maintainers of social order. *The prophets were disruptors of social consensus. Within the system there is inherent conflict but, ideally, also a balance.*[84]

This is an apt description of Kit's role. The movement named here reveals her spirituality, her way to God. She was a disrupter of the social compass. And this drive was a core part of her being, a defining factor of her spirituality. Some markings in the Chapter 2000 document revealed elements of her spirituality. The first paragraph Kit

[83] Marie-Louise Wolfington, RSCJ, born in Philadelphia on 10/7/1931, former member of Kit's community and advancement director in several schools.

[84] Taken from *Prophets: Self Critical Thinking* by Richard Rohr, OFM., Center for Action and Contemplation.

marked is in the opening Conference of Patricia García de Quevedo, superior general, in which she names scenarios that called to new signs, challenging and mobilizing the Society. The first theme was near and dear to Kit's heart: Globalization.

> Globalization is a reality that affects our life in a positive sense through the strength of our internationality, lived as a resource and challenge, facilitating better communication and deepening the experience of solidarity among us and with others. But we are also aware of the negative consequences of globalization: increased poverty, exclusion, violence and war.[85]

Kit experienced the world as one, and her spirituality reflected this. She knew instinctively that to be faithful to the vision of Saint Madeleine Sophie, the Society had to adapt to the needs of the times and to do things differently from the way they had been done in the past. The Chapter 2000 articulated it this way:

> We need to open ourselves so as to receive the contributions of different cultures—of Asia and Africa, of other faith traditions, of other currents of thought and action like eco-feminism. All of these will give us a vision of education as a work of co-creation. Thus, we will recognize the Spirit who carries out and who pours out her wisdom on us in the act of giving birth.
>
> What are the challenges that need to be discerned, so as to define the Society's priorities for the coming years? The projects of the provinces suggest some:
>
> - Offering an alternative education in a globalized world, which builds on the positive aspects of globalization;
>
> - Offering an education in our institutions that develops the capacity to discern values and to evaluate our practice with a view to accept or reject what the situation and circumstances impose;
>
> - Collaborating with other groups so as to come to a more open and deeper relationship with lay people.

[85] General Chapter 2000, English version, p. 7.

All her life, Kit had been doing this, in the Network, at the CEDC, in the United States and abroad. The key for Kit was collaboration. Chapter 2000 confirmed and affirmed the need for this way of being and doing. This section on collaboration was the one that Kit most underlined:

> We discover, live and announce God's love, which is at the heart of our charism. This impels us to work together and with others in partnership to foster life and to contribute to the building of an alternative society.

Ministering in the schools, starting the Network, working in the CEDC, Kit had collaborated with RSCJ and colleagues, learning from all of them, discovering new possibilities together:

> Collaboration implies team building, delegating and assuming our co-responsibility for the common good, working on common projects and developing together new processes in our service of education. In order to have reciprocal relationships with our co-workers, whether we are in a position of authority or not, whether in a work sponsored by the Society or not, we need to allow our perspectives to be transformed by the outlook of others while remaining true to our own values (Chapter 2000, English translation, page 27).

Intellectually, Kit knew this was the ideal of collaboration, but she struggled with allowing her perspectives to be transformed. Often she believed her perspective was the only accurate one. Georgie Blaeser found that "You could not win a fight with her." Meg Canty and Anne Dyer, both dear friends, admitted that she was stubborn. Perhaps it was her struggle to live and act in a collaborative way that led her to "star" the following sections of Chapter 2000:

> We are called to be profoundly collaborative at different levels: in daily life, with our neighbors, in our work place, in our local, provincial and interprovincial communities.

> We walk with our lay sisters and brothers as baptized members of the Church and as citizens in society, conscious at the same time of our specific gift and responsibilities.

Kit did not keep journals or diaries that would trace her spiritual journey. Asked to describe Kit's spirituality, Nance O'Neil wrote in 2020, ten years after her death:

> Kit could find God anywhere. I know that and I suspect the reverse is also true. In Maine lobsters? Really? In her brother's sensitivity and care for his special son? Yes, as diverse as that. She was definitely not pious in the common sense of the word but God was real to her even in the dark days after her heart attack during her aspirantship. She believed God has a sense of humor too. And could come up with a quote from Scripture which would prove it when we shared our lives of prayer.
>
> When the idea of a technology center for media communication began to surface and the provincial team thought the Province could/should try to start one, whose name surfaced? Kit's. She had mid-wived the Network of Sacred Heart Schools, and if you're looking for spirituality, look at the base for the Network. She had a vision for that which was not yet complete so when I broached the idea of what eventually became the CEDC, she said it was a good idea but vehemently explained why it was not for her. The morning after we talked about the media ministry, the reading at the PH community prayer was the rich young man. After prayer, Kit came to me with tears in her eyes and said "I don't want to go away sad. If you need me to do it, I will."[86]

Kit was a very social being, so for her going to God was a community affair. She knew she could not go to God alone. Her family and friends were part of the fabric of her spirituality. Her closest friends in the Society were Mickey McKay, Nance O'Neil, and Rosemary (Ronnie) Dewey. They met faithfully to share honestly and courageously. Nance commented on the "Foursome":

> I'd think the foursome might deserve a bit more elaboration. We saw each other through some rough spots for thirty years or more until Mickey died. Then the three of us continued. When Mickey—or later, I—was out of the country, we still

[86] Nance O'Neil, letter to the writer

met as three. We got together two or three times a year and shared where we were (or weren't) with God in our lives and ministries. When I think of community, this is what I hope our communities can do.

Inherent in Kit's being was her desire to build communion wherever she found herself. Her friends, like her family, were extremely important to Kit and to her spiritual growth. She was a people-person, and went to God through them. Ann Taylor[87] characterized Kit as a "frontier spirit.…. People were sacraments of God for Kit." She enjoyed people and received life from them. As Susan Maxwell said of Kit, "Her life was its own best witness."

Kit lived in Washington, D.C., for twenty-eight years. She knew the city inside and out, had numerous friends and acquaintances, and relished the intrigue of life there. For twenty-five years, Kit lived with Betsy Hartson. Betsy remembered Kit's life as "so full of creativity, energy, depth, and passion." She remembered their initial meeting at Kenwood:

> Kit and I were in the noviceship together. Kit was my angel, which may not be a very appropriate name for someone with Kit's personality, sense of humor and gifts as a leader. When I entered, I knew nothing about cloister and the life of poverty, of having two outfits, and a rule of silence. I made it through the noviceship, probably because of her spirit. I am very grateful for her in my life. She focused on others and their situation and their needs, making them feel more at home in the new environment. Her leadership skills and ability to make others feel good and important about what they were doing and where they were doing it has always been a part of her thinking. Over the years, Kit and I kept up with each other in spite of living in different provinces; we met together and worked on committees and new projects.

[87] Ann Taylor, RSCJ, born in Boston on 1/21/1939, former headmistress and longtime chair of SHCOG of the USC Province.

Betsy's memories continue:

> In 1991, when I was leaving my ministry with the young professed, Kit suggested that I come to DC and she would find me a ministry with the homeless, work that interested me. She found me a ministry and also found a house in Brookland where we ended up starting a new community.

They lived in that house on Otis Street in Washington, D.C., for nineteen years until Kit's death in 2010. The Society had bought the house in 1991 from a widow who loved hats. When she sold the house, she left some of the hats in the attic. The community called her about the hats, and she said to keep them. This led to parties hosted by Kit and Betsy. At the gatherings, each guest was given a hat to wear when she arrived. Just the picture of a group of nuns or colleagues, sitting in the living room, wearing hats evokes smiles, if not laughter.

According to Betsy:

> Kit was not only wise, determined and creative but also a unique leader. Working with her, you felt that you were the one who had succeeded or accomplished a task or project with her support. But the reality was that her brains and creativity behind it were essential to success. She became acquainted with many non-profit organizations in DC and in Maryland and she was well connected with many religious orders. She was asked to work with them on major issues.
>
> I started working at a homeless family center and then with Catholic Charities Homeless services, which was the move that lead to our founding Living Wages Adult Education Center, which has been in existence since 1999. Kit supported our program from the beginning with the CEDC creating a logo, which was recognized for its excellence. She also gave us a place to meet and retreat days with Living Wages staff and volunteers.

Kit was an encourager in Betsy's life but also the person with connections who could make things happen. She was an enterprising and imaginative force behind the beginnings of Living Wages, a non-profit organization that prepares participants to become life-long learners, to compete in the job market and take their place in the workplace.

One of the co-founders of Living Wages, Robert Crittenden, classified Kit as a "unique person" who made a lasting impression and who had strong experiences. Bob said Kit was very supportive of the work of the organization. She took pictures of graduation and the Christmas party. Bob recalled,

> Kit had her staff design our logo, design our website and web page. Kit was very proud of her Irish heritage, and in loving fun, called me "Roberto" to emphasize my Italian ancestry. Sometimes, she would actually give in to me, by saying, "All right, Roberto, have it your way."

Aisha Monroe, another employee at Living Wages, remembers Kit as "authentic, open and faithful." Kit was "faithful to her commitment and presence to everyone. She met people where they were, and never talked down to anyone."

Serving was a huge factor in Kit's life. She was chosen as area director of the RSCJ community in Washington, D.C., for two terms, 2003–2009. An area director was the person charged with the functioning of one of the geographical locations of RSCJ in the United States Province. She was given authority by the provincial team and by the members of the area to exercise leadership and to coordinate the responsibilities entrusted to the area community. Nominated by the members of the area, Kit was appointed by the provincial team. The reasons given for her nomination reveal aspects of Kit's personality. Among the traits cited:

- [Kit] Has the ability to motivate a group; would take the job seriously
- Would be great at this. She has creative ideas and energy. She is also a very caring person, who will be supportive when those in the area need her to be. It will also give her a chance to use positive energy within the area, as opposed to "negative energy." She is strong, and I think…we need that. She has not done this before and that brings new and fresh ideas.
- Kit has a great sense of humor, a deep commitment to the Society, and a big and loving heart.
- I believe that she will be a good director because she is creative, innovative, and is a good listener.

- Has vision and gifts for leadership; is creative, organized, has a deep love of the Society and has had experience working with the wider Society.
- Kit is a woman of strong faith, love for the mission of our Society, and genuine compassion for others.... Kit brings vision into our lives; helps us....
- I have known Kit for many years and I see her as a strong leader, a creative talented person. She uses her gifts for the good of the Society and for all those around her.... She sees what is possible, and is tireless in pursuing goals. I believe she is a leader in the classic sense and I name her with confidence.

In 1987-88, Kit was one of the nominees for provincial of the United States Province. The pros and cons for nominating Kit were well stated by one RSCJ who focused on Kit's strengths and weaknesses. Reflecting on the state of the province and Kit's ability to assume this position, she painted a vivid picture of Kit as a person:

> With these thoughts as a background, I nominate Catherine Collins as our next provincial. Kit is outstanding for her creative vision, her intelligence, her understanding of the reality in which we live and which we are called to serve. She has thought deeply about what it means to "seek justice with the heart of an educator"—she is an educator *par excellence*. She has a deep loyalty to the Society and an understanding of our life on all levels—local, provincial, national, and international. Of anyone in the Society, she is most in touch with all five provinces in the United States because of her work as national coordinator for the schools. She has been a part of the Interprovincial Board as a staff member for the last five years or so and has the ability, I think, to be a catalyst in the effort to resolve the national reorganization question. Her administrative skills are made more valuable by the creativity and clear thinking they implement.
>
> On a deeper level, Kit is woman who has met God in loneliness, in physical suffering, in misunderstanding, as well as in joy and in laughter. She has a profound sense of mystery, of call, of destiny, and I have been privileged to meet her and be with her in faith in the Lord's presence. She has integrated her life and lives it with enthusiasm and humor that both inspire and delight.

I am a person no longer involved in our schools. After thirteen happy years spent in four of them, I left them to teach poor children. (The parochial school where I teach now is, I think, today's expression of Saint Madeleine Sophie's poor school). Despite my orientation and my realization that Kit's total involvement in our institutions gives her a vested interest in their survival as well as an understanding of "corporateness" that differs from mine, I think she is what we need now. The issues we are facing now are huge: they go beyond province boundaries.

Kit is not the "mothering" type. If people are looking for someone who will spend her energies focusing on *us* as individuals and communities, she will probably not meet their expectations. But I think we are beyond the state of being concerned about our own needs—we need her challenge and vision to take us beyond ourselves, to get us focused *outwardly*.

In the end, the superior general did not name Kit provincial nor was she chosen for the provincial team. Rosemary Bearss wrote to Kit:

From reading the nominations, it is obvious to me that you are valued and trusted by a significant number in the Province. Enclosed is a summary listing of the qualities that were named as yours. Each comment listed here was articulated in different ways and was repeated many times....

Even though some members saw Kit as aspiring to be provincial, yet many recognized that her vision and gifts were needed in other areas of the province—strategic planning, developing organizational schemas, and working with the various groups that the Center served. She remained at the Center.

By 1996, the provincial team, her coworkers, and community members were growing concerned about Kit's mental and physical health. Kit identified with her work and refused to be accountable. The staff especially was concerned about her need to control agenda. The provincial team felt that Kit needed to leave the Center, take time off, and take care of herself. The problem was how to make this happen. In the end, there was no intervention, and nothing changed. When asked,

team members were nervous about confronting her. A new provincial and team were named, and Kit's life went on as usual.[88]

In the summer of 2007, at the province assembly, it was noticeable to many that something was wrong with Kit. When she went to the microphone to represent an opinion or express an idea, she was unable to speak coherently. Members of the province expressed their concern to the provincial team, and the staff at the Center wrote innumerable notes to the team expressing concern for Kit.

The Otis Street Community had a Saint Patrick's Day party in 2010. This was one of Kit's favorite holidays, and she even prepared the potatoes! On the day following the big party, Kit did not go to the Center. This was not unusual, for some mornings she did not go to the office. However, when she did not answer either her cell phone or the house phone, the staff became alarmed. Will Simpson called Betsy Hartson, Kit's long-time community member, and together they drove to Otis Street. Betsy, sensing something was terribly wrong, stayed downstairs, while Will went upstairs. There he found Kit dead. Her death was the result of her ongoing battle with heart disease. She was seventy-three.

The email notice sent to the religious stunned not only the province, but the whole international Society. Condolences poured in. While Betsy was calling Kit's family, others were calling the RSCJ. The provincial, Paula Toner, reached the motherhouse in Rome. Paula then called Clare Pratt, the director of the retirement community in Atherton, California, and a lifelong friend of Kit's. When Clare answered the phone, Paula asked, "Are you sitting down?" Julie Yachtis volunteered for phone duty and quickly realized that each caller was brimming over with a "Kit story," whether from the previous week or fifty years earlier.

Although stunned and grieving, the RSCJ moved into planning the funeral. Betsy Hartson and Vicky Rajca determined that Kit would have wanted to be buried in Washington, among her religious sisters there. Kit deeply loved the Washington area, both RSCJ and the city; and a month before her death, she had told the religious that Washington had long ago become her "home." The Center she created, where Kit worked and reached out to the city, was chosen as the place for the wake and funeral.

Kit's close friend, Tracy Gray, and her husband, John, began to help

[88] Unpublished notes of provincial team 1996.

by cleaning and preparing the Otis Street community house for Kit's family to stay there with Betsy. Vicky Rajca galvanized the staff at the Center into action to transform the room that had become a storeroom back to a sacred space. As Betsy said, "It was so fitting that Kit's wake and Mass take place not just at the Center, but in the chapel where so many holy RSCJ had prayed in past years."

The liturgy was a glorious celebration of Kit's life. George Williams, SJ, who knew Kit well and had often celebrated liturgies with Kit's community, said he considered it a privilege to be the presider. Just as in life, in death Kit brought various types of people together. The CEDC designed the funeral program and memory card. Anne Dyer and Will Simpson gave the eulogies. The music included Kit's request for "How Can I Keep from Singing" and "Danny Boy." It was wonderful to have Clare Pratt, Meg Canty, and Will Simpson's wife, Ave Luke Simpson, to lead, cantor, and solo, with Richard Fazio, husband of a Stone Ridge faculty member, accompanying.

Representatives from the many communities to which Kit belonged offered the Prayer of the Faithful. Nieces, nephews, and co-workers were among those bringing up gifts and serving as pallbearers. Jim Hug, SJ, associated with Center for Concern, proclaimed the Gospel, while George in his homily spoke not only about Kit personally but also called everyone to a deep faith-filled reflection on the Paschal Mystery and Risen Life.

Although Kit's brother, Joe, was too ill to attend, her sister Polly was present, along with George; Joe's wife Susan; and many of Kit's nieces and nephews and their children. The sharing of memories, a recent RSCJ practice and part of the wake, clearly demonstrated that Kit's characteristic passion and wit ran through three generations! The family told humorous stories of her, and laughter filled the rooms. In addition to the RSCJ in the Washington area, guests came from all over the country: Georgie Blaeser, Marie Buonato, Grace Butler, Mavie Coakley, Fran de la Chapelle, Ronnie Dewey, Bunny Flick, Judy Garson, Kathleen Hughes, Ann Jablonski, Maggie Kilduff, Joan Kirby, Mary Helen McComas, Cecile Meijer, Barbara Moreau, Clare Pratt, and Ann Taylor. Other guests included persons from the neighborhood, the Morino organization, Living Wages, Stone Ridge, Manhattanville; Kit's college roommate, Susan Murphy; Malin Craig's sister, Connie Craig, SHCJ; and religious of other congregations. The attendees were numerous and varied, attesting to Kit's life and legacy.

Kit was very much present at this farewell. She would have thoroughly enjoyed it, and her Irish eyes must have been smiling. Even those in her family who radically disagreed with her politics readily agreed about how delighted Kit would have been with the Mass of Resurrection celebrated for her, which significantly took place the day the Affordable Care Act (Obamacare) was signed into law.

Anne Dyer, Kit's lifelong friend and colleague, gave a eulogy that beautifully summarized Kit's life:

> Fifty odd years ago, Kit Collins with many of us here today, was in the noviceship at Kenwood. At a certain point Kit was the bell ringer. None of us realized it at the time, but I think it was a metaphor of things to come. I think she was much more than a bell ringer. I think she was a bellwether—the sheep that wears a bell around its neck and goes before the flock and announces its whereabouts. Kit was always out in front. She was a visionary, an educator and, above all, a storyteller.
>
> As a visionary, the Council doors of Vatican II had barely closed when Kit was talking about how we needed to be one province of the Society in the United States. She voraciously read everything that came from that council and, much to the dismay of some of her sisters, wanted to implement immediately—NOW! The same was true when we concluded our own Special Chapter of 1967. It was in those years of the late 1960s and early 1970s that she developed her commitment to the poor, the underdog and voiceless. A friend and admirer of Father Horace McKenna, she made certain that the resources of Stone Ridge would be available to the opening of the ministry of Sursum Corda, a subsidized housing project for the poor in Washington, D.C. Beds, linens, furniture—all went straight from the recently closed boarding school at Stone Ridge in Bethesda to the newly formed community in the city. ...
>
> Kit also saw the coming of the digital age and understood the power that would be unleashed by technology in the field of communications. Faithful to her life as an educator, she founded the Center for Educational Design and Communication. It was at the Center that she truly found her home and her passion, and gave a voice to those who might otherwise have remained silent. Situated in the heart of the city, she could live and walk among the poor, attend

every protest, march for the rights of the oppressed, and make regular forays to Capitol Hill to enter into the eye of the hurricane of Washington politics, a sport she truly enjoyed.

As an educator, Kit was at home with both children and adults. She chaired the International Education Commission for the Society of the Sacred Heart. She gave voice to the *Goals and Criteria* in Australia, New Zealand, much of the Far East, Africa, and Europe and was a leader in the design and construction of *An Act of Hope*, a document that had repercussions around the globe. Kit envisioned Sacred Heart education having a real impact on the world. She saw everything as connected—"Network" was much more than just an image; it was organized entanglement, and for her relationships and bonds lasted forever.

Kit was a profoundly spiritual person in a truly non-traditional way. She had a theology for everything—for education, for community, for communication. That meant she could find God anywhere and everywhere. I especially enjoyed her theology of the airport. And this, of course, lost nothing in the telling.

Above all, Kit was a storyteller. The stories were not about herself, but the mundane events of life that could become the highlight of someone's day. She could see the ludicrous in the most prosaic of circumstances and could make people laugh until tears ran down their cheeks. She had a knack for mimicry and was a master of the fine art of hyperbole.

Here there is a great temptation to tell some of the stories, but to each one I suggested, someone said, "No, you can't say that in Church," so those stories will have to be saved for a later time—maybe with our wine and cheese.

Nevertheless, I can imagine her at this moment regaling God with the story of her arrival into heaven and entering into a discussion on the theology of funerals. And if we listen closely, we might even hear a faint tinkle of a bell.

The author of Kit's circular letter (a brief biography sent to all RSCJ) wrote: "Occasionally, there appears among us a woman, whose vision and the power to implement it alter our understanding of our apostolate and our manner of carrying it out." This was Kit Collins.

She was "ahead of her time, but the effect of her life and work brought us into the future she envisioned."

Tributes poured in. Some were from the people at the Morino Institute:

> I loved to share a scotch with her from time to time. She was one of a kind, and one of the kindest, most sincere people I have ever met. I am truly heartbroken.

> Kit was one of the most transformational, visionary, inclusive, and effective leaders and mentors of my personal and professional life.

> I loved her big vision and creative mind – what a loss

> Kit made such an important contribution to the Education Commission and to this day the 'grey book', fruit of their work is still being used in different parts of the Society. She was also so generous in accepting tasks that, as Central Team, we confided to her. Her work with us as a Team helped to move us forward; her facilitation was clear, spiced with her delightful sense of humor and very effective. Kit was the courageous pioneer who helped us set up the Network of Sacred Heart Schools in this province and in others, and in addition, set up twenty-first century communication systems for the whole Society.

> I am deeply saddened by this news. I had the honor of knowing and working with Kit, who was amazing. I had some real fun doing some "give back" work, fixing kitchen equipment at the conference center she was a part of. Every time I expressed some doubt about being able to fix something, she always gave me that 'I know you can' look which made me try harder. Her spirit and spirituality taught me a lot then and continues to teach me today. This is a huge loss.

> It is the rare people like her that provide an example for how we should try to live our lives. She blessed so many with her life's work.

> And we all have to be thankful that we got to know and learn from someone as special as Sister Kit. She was, and will continue to be, such an inspiration, and I will always remember her with her luminous smile and a Red Sox hat.

> I know she would want us to celebrate her life by remembering how she made us reflect on what is truly

important. And, of course, how she made us laugh until our sides hurt.

I did not know Kit as well as you all, of course, but from the first time I met her I found her delightful. One of my favorite memories of her is at a birthday party where we were. I looked over and Kit had a big cigar clenched in her teeth, a stiff drink in her hand, and was delightfully taking in the action. She could talk sports, politics, religion…you name it. We'll miss her because the world was a better place with her in it.

Kit Collins was an apostle of newness, demonstrating a constant timeliness, creativity, and the effectiveness of love for the Society of the Sacred Heart by her life and activities. From her we can learn to integrate creativity and innovation. For Kit it was not enough to pray, "Thy kingdom come," but it was necessary to work so that the kingdom of God lives vibrantly among us today. Kit was a change agent, never content with the status quo. She envisioned the Network of Sacred Heart Schools, not separate schools. Leaving the Network, the Center for Educational Design and Communication was her next undertaking. Her influence affected not only the United States, but also the international scene.

Photo on Memorial card for Kit Collins

By the time of her death in 2010, she had become an important figure in the life of the Religious of the Sacred Heart and their lay

CATHERINE COLLINS, RSCJ (1937 – 2010)

colleagues in the United States. Perhaps what she is best remembered for today is the Network of Sacred Heart Schools, an organization of excellent schools all committed to the same philosophy of education expressed in a common set of goals. Her vision lives in every Sacred Heart school and within the Society. Barbara Dawson presents a picture of Kit calling, leading us into the future.

> I often wish that Kit were still alive. Sometimes I find myself saying "I wonder what Kit would think about this?" Of course, we did not always agree, but I probably had some of the most interesting and challenging conversations with her about the Society's mission, the changing role of RSCJ, our partnerships with our lay colleagues, how the whole Society could be organized differently and more organically. It was so energizing to sit on the back porch of her house or at the Stuart Center and work together on how the future could be better. She would want us to continue the conversation!

Printed in the United States
by Baker & Taylor Publisher Services